Book Reviews for 'Fc _____ inter

'*From her childhood adventures to her dedicated life as a psychic medium, Liz Winter takes you on a journey through her life of exploration, learning and communication with Spirit. Interwoven with her compassion and service to others, Liz's life story sparkles with love and humour. Written with Liz's natural warmth and grace—it is an absolute joy to read.*'

Robyn Sutcliffe,
Eagle Proofreading

'*Books on spirit communication and the presence of 'other worlds' are hard to deliver to a wide audience because it's an area that is outside of most people's own experience . . . . and comfort zone. But as you read Liz Winter's warm and candid book, you cannot help but like her and more importantly, you get a sense right from the beginning, that she is someone you can trust. She writes so fluidly and without any pretence about her life experiences, you feel you are right there with her as her fascinating account unfolds. Her grounded common sense, her innate kindness and the clarity of her abilities are all very evident, as is the advice she is able to offer from her unique perspective as a bridge between worlds. Her explanation of the these worlds and the reassurance it brings is a welcome message indeed.*'

Jeddah Mali,
International Mentor & Advisor—
Global Paradigm Ltd

Each word I read and page I turned I felt a deeper connection to this courageous woman as she so beautifully held my virtual hand and guided me through her early years and forward sharing her memories and realizations that brought her to become the amazing woman she is today. Liz Winter will touch your heart and soul with her passion for her true calling and assist you with connecting to Spirit. Most definitely there was divine plan followed here and many will be touched by her grace, compassion, connection with Spirit and abundant joy.

Kelly A. Chamchuk—
Author, Soul Coach @ www.LumaSoul.com

For the Love of Spirit

A Medium Memoir

Liz Winter

BALBOA.
PRESS

A DIVISION OF HAY HOUSE

Balboa Press books may be ordered through booksellers or by contacting:

Balboa Press
A Division of Hay House
1663 Liberty Drive
Bloomington, IN 47403
www.balboapress.com.au
1-(877) 407-4847

ISBN: 978-1-4525-1046-0 (sc)
ISBN: 978-1-4525-1049-1 (e)

Because of the dynamic nature of the Internet, any web addresses or links contained in this book may have changed since publication and may no longer be valid. The views expressed in this work are solely those of the author and do not necessarily reflect the views of the publisher, and the publisher hereby disclaims any responsibility for them.

The author of this book does not dispense medical advice or prescribe the use of any technique as a form of treatment for physical, emotional, or medical problems without the advice of a physician, either directly or indirectly. The intent of the author is only to offer information of a general nature to help you in your quest for emotional and spiritual well-being. In the event you use any of the information in this book for yourself, which is your constitutional right, the author and the publisher assume no responsibility for your actions.

Any people depicted in stock imagery provided by Thinkstock are models, and such images are being used for illustrative purposes only.
Certain stock imagery © Thinkstock.

Printed in the United States of America

Balboa Press rev. date: 06/05/2013

For Jono

Contents

Introduction

For the Love of Spirit was born one summer morning as I awoke from slumber. I sensed the presence of my Spirit Guide, White Owl. I heard his familiar voice in my head say, *It is time to tell your story, how you became a channel for Spirit.*

I began to argue: 'But I want to write self-help books, White Owl, I don't want to write about me!'

'Later, little one; please trust. First you must tell your story, and we want you to call it *For the Love of Spirit*'.

Within seconds the energy in the room was normal again, and I knew he had gone. I was left with a feeling of euphoria and an overwhelming feeling of joy. I knew in my heart I would follow White Owl's direction.

So began the journey. My wish is that through reading my story, you are touched by the Spirit realm and are inspired to believe that you truly are loved by invisible forces.

If not for the love of Spirit in my life, I would not be as happy as I am, right here and right now.

My prayers and blessings go out to all who hold this book.

With heartfelt love, Liz

'White Owl' Spirit Drawing by Marion Ruffin

Chapter 1

Crossroads

The violet glow of the morning sun crept gently through my bedroom window on a blustery, cool day in 1974. This would be the last time I would awake in this room. Today we were leaving.

Mum and I packed up the house. We worked quickly, and the long white moving truck arrived at the perfect time. Dad was at work and he didn't know. By lunchtime, we crammed, relieved and exhausted, into the tan-coloured EH Holden. As we drove down the road, I turned my thirteen-year-old head around to catch a final glimpse of our home. I felt a rush of excitement rather than sadness, and I turned to my mother to share the feeling. But I saw a tear gently falling down her soft, red cheek. In my young mind I couldn't understand and I asked, 'Mum, why are you crying?'

She looked at me with her green, weary eyes as she ran a hand through her dark hair and said, 'You can't be married to someone for twenty-five years, have seven children, and feel nothing'.

In my simple innocence, I said, 'But now you won't have to argue all the time and you will be happy'.

Mum turned her eyes back to the road and said nothing. I noticed the corners of her mouth began to turn upward, just slightly, and I relaxed inside, hoping that perhaps what I had just said had sunk in. She was probably smiling at my simple perspective.

I looked out the car window as we passed familiar landmarks like the corner shop, the park, and the school I would now be leaving. I began to see scenes in my mind from my childhood that had all been part of who I was now and where I was going. The memories faded in and out between the fantasies of where we were going and what life would be like without my Dad. I remembered guiltily how I had run away from home the previous summer with a girl from up the road. It was a spontaneous act with no real plan. I'd had a terrible argument with my parents. I had run to my bedroom, and without knowing why, I grabbed three pair of underpants and my diary. A clear voice in my head cautioned me that now was a time for patience, not for rash actions, but I ignored it. I often heard voices and sometimes I listened and sometimes I didn't. I then ran to my girlfriend's house on the next block, and before we knew it, we were hitchhiking up the Hume Highway to Sydney. The police brought us home five days later, and we were grounded for weeks. I regretted the worry and pain I had caused my family, but I'd had such an urge to search for something and didn't have a clue what I was looking for.

As it turned out, in the coming weeks after we left Dad, Mum and I were the happiest we had ever been. We set up a flat together, and there was finally peace in the home. One of my brothers chose to stay on with Dad, and not surprisingly, he reported that Dad did get a shock that evening when he arrived home. I only saw my father a few times after that before his death in 1984.

That was a major turning point in my life, with many more to come.

Perhaps the most important turning point for all of us is arriving here in the physical world. I arrived here on earth one spring afternoon when cherry blossoms lined the streets and floral breezes filled the air. It was 1961.

I was three weeks late. My skin was red and peeling, and my reluctance to exit the safety of my mother's womb had caused frustration to many, including the doctor. Quite peeved he had been called in on a Saturday, the good doctor greeted me with a violent slap to my bottom and literally threw me in the air to my mother's open arms. 'You wanted a girl', he said. 'Here she is!' And with that, he abruptly left, leaving the nurses to clean up and my parched mother waiting for a cup of tea that never arrived.

There were no prophets present, no seers or psychics to warn my mother that her newly born daughter was one day to communicate with the dead. Instead, I was dragged off to a cold, loveless nursery, as was the custom, and separated from the nurturing woman who had carried me in her body all those months. My soul was now in a physical body, and any recent memories of where I had come from were erased. The separation from source and mother had begun.

Like someone who has lost her sense of sight and hearing, I was left with only instincts to guide my path ahead. Of course it starts like that for all of us, until eventually we return to the same forgotten place, unless we are fortunate to stumble across a portal to our source during our brief time here. I am one of those fortunate people.

The geographic location of my birth was in the cosmopolitan city of Melbourne. I have always admired Melbourne for its sense of rawness. The place has an edge about it. Maybe it is the distinct and extreme seasons of its southerly setting or perhaps because it tends to attract a large cross-section of different people. There is an authenticity in the way people relate there and a bluntness about the place that is very grounding, albeit sometimes depressing. A unique code of dry humour exists amongst Melbournians and they can smell a phoney a mile away. It was to serve me well growing up in such a blunt and grounding city.

I was the youngest of seven children. My mother, Violet, has often told me the story about when she was six months pregnant with me. Mum had to hide me under her warm coat in the bitterly cold winter. My family had relocated from Morwell, a country town in Victoria, and were seeking rental accommodation. While my dad was at work at a tyre factory, she would catch trams, trains, and buses with my other siblings looking for somewhere to live. My mother figured seven children might just be the final straw to a potential landlord.

Not long before I was born, she secured a rental property in the suburb of Essendon North. It was a huge, somewhat spooky one-hundred-year-old house. The rent was seventeen pounds a week. In hindsight, it was a perfect location for a teenage horror movie. Located across the road from the major airport, the house was once a small, private hospital and also a riding school. The foundations of the house were made from bluestone, and the external walls were rendered brick. The front entrance had a tall, cast-iron fence with sharp ends pointing to the sky. Its peeling white paint revealed its fading demise. I still remember the deep tone of the screech that gate made whilst swinging on it, waiting for the postman to arrive with his whistle. There were elegant grey stone steps leading up to a broad verandah. The French-looking doors had huge stained-glass panels that were created using swirling shades of blue, yellow, and crimson in delicately placed patterns. In a way, the house resembled a small castle. There were five bedrooms, a long passageway, and high ceilings with intricate, cobwebbed roof cornices. Worn, olive-green linoleum covered the floors while peeling wallpaper of various floral designs adorned the walls. In its day, it would have been an elegant and impressive piece of real estate, but it had long been neglected. It was perfect for a large and growing family, and my parents were greatly relieved when they found this unique and affordable home.

The house was freezing cold in winter but a cool oasis during the hot summer. Artful, old-fashioned fireplaces with marble mantelpieces featured in each room, and my mother would often hang a cloth over them to prevent the breezes coming down the chimneys. Second-hand furniture was scattered throughout the house, and although my mother worked hard to keep it clean, the dust would settle as quickly as she could remove it.

Down a spiral staircase, under the house, was a huge cellar that I found both frightening and fascinating. The foreboding, heavy white door heralded the entrance to the basement, which was usually securely bolted. Our parents didn't like us going down there, which of course only served to make it more enticing to a child.

The feelings of adrenalin and excitement when we were permitted to enter the cellar stairway were exhilarating. The first thing I would notice was the drop in temperature and a deep silence, coupled with butterflies in my stomach. I would run my hand along the rounded bluestone wall as I gingerly took another step down. A whisper became an echo, and the distortion of senses produced a type of natural high. I felt fear, but a good fear, the sort of fear that is exciting and almost addictive. The basement had a round floor plan and contained several bay windows at ground level. Looking up at the world through those bay windows unleashed a new perspective and set my imagination on fire. Stories of the past were buried in the walls of that cellar, and although one could not see or hear them, a sensitive person could feel them.

Outside was a vast garden with rundown wooden fences that you could exit and enter through if you chose to. In a side garden was a line of fragrant peppercorn trees, with slightly twisted trunks and strong branches. I loved climbing them and picking the felt-like leaves so I could crush them in my tiny hands to release the sweet scent that would bombard my senses. They were laden with lime-green caterpillars, cylinder-shaped cocoons, black and red ladybugs, and the occasional mysteriously built birds' nests. Many a time I needed help to climb down after being lost in my imagination for hours.

I loved the tall, majestic pine tree that would lose a branch each Christmas for our tree, as there was never enough money to buy one. The pine tree also served as a landmark if I got lost in the nearby streets, as I could always see it and navigate my way home.

Regardless of our poverty, there was always a healthy supply of shiny black briquettes in Hessian bags sitting outside the back kitchen door. I can still smell and feel their chalky texture when I would place them in the metal bucket and drag their heavy weight inside.

Unless the fire was lit, there was no hot water, and an ancient wood-burning stove sat in the kitchen corner. An old-fashioned water tower, which once would have been the water supply to the house, stood tall outside the kitchen window. There was also a well that had been filled in with dirt. There seemed to be endless nooks and crannies inside and outside that a child could get lost in.

Long before the days of computers and mobile phones, my siblings and I spent many hours playing outdoors, chasing chooks and climbing trees. I recall being horrified when a chook was beheaded for a Sunday roast after church, although my brothers thought it was hilarious to watch the body run around without a head. The harsher side of life is inevitably exposed in our young lives at some point for all of us. It shocks us out of the moment.

When a child realises the world is not always predictable, loving, and safe, it is then that a child may begin to wonder what life is really about. As a child, I often felt a growing sense of discomfort but couldn't really articulate why.

There were lush plum, apricot, and blackberry trees that bore perfect fruit for a summer treat as well as the occasional stomach-ache. The sky was wide and the Melbourne air was crisp. Lying on my back on the thick green grass, I would daydream as I watched clouds pass and aeroplanes fly over, arriving and taking off from the airport across the road. I wondered where people were going, and I would wave and I thought they could see me.

A huge loganberry tree had grown in a bent-over fashion, and I used it as a round cubby house where I would often play and hide. Large mushrooms grew nearby, and I believed they housed fairies and would leave presents out for them. Even then, as now, my own space was important to me. When I was in my cubby house I was free to create, free to feel, free to cry, and free to just be me without competing with siblings or parents or having to act the way I was expected to.

At some point our family acquired a black-and-white television. It sat in the corner almost like an altar of fascination, and we would argue over what program to watch. My two sisters and I were outnumbered by our four brothers, so they often won with Sunday afternoon wrestling. I loved watching anything that had an element of magic like *Disneyland* or *Bewitched*.

When I was ten years old we had our first telephone connected. How I loved that telephone. It was a creamy white colour with an old-fashioned dial face that felt wonderful and made a shrill sound when you dialled a number. I would sit in front of it admiring it for hours, longing for it to ring, and always raced to answer it. At that point it was simply incomprehensible that there would come a day in my lifetime that we could have our own personal, mobile telephone.

There was even a granny flat, which was originally used to house servants, attached to the house. Boarders often lived there helping to supplement my parents' income. I remember the granny flat toilet had a golden cord you would pull to flush it, and as a young child I thought it was very grand.

One of the beauties of not having much is that it tends to teach one the art of resourcefulness. I remember using cardboard boxes to make myself a new bedroom table or making up a game straight from my imagination. The way we lived was what would be called 'green' now. Mum would darn socks, recycle leftover chicken to make a pot of soup, and feed scraps to the chooks.

I was often bullied at school, as I was one of the 'poor' kids. We never had much and I wore hand-me-down clothes from my older siblings, which were often the cause of cruel remarks from other children. I found it hard to make friends. Somehow you just carried on. It wasn't like now when there is so much awareness of children's issues. Children really were still meant to be seen and not heard.

The public State School we attended was very old-fashioned and strict. Boys were strapped for the smallest of misdemeanours and I copped the odd slap of the hands and the ruler behind the legs. I remember discovering the emotion 'compassion' when a boy in first class was strapped simply because he interrupted while the teacher was talking. Red welts appeared on his hands as he tried so hard to not cry. I didn't particularly like the boy. I just knew and felt that that was unnecessary violence.

However, the physical abuse was probably not as damaging as the fear the teachers would instil. We had to march in military fashion in the courtyard, singing the national anthem, and woe betide you if you fell out of step or forgot the words. I remember being slapped in the first grade because I didn't write a capital letter in a story we were writing. I truly believed I was a bad person. Another memory is getting into trouble for finishing my work too quickly. I realise now that I was quite a bright student, but it was never acknowledged.

I recently revisited the school for the first time in forty-odd years, on a public holiday, and stood outside the gate realising it was not half as big as I remembered it to be. It was a full moon that day, and the sunlight seemed exceptionally bright. It was an illuminating moment for me standing there. The school had changed somewhat but still had many of the original buildings, and I saw the dreaded quadrangle where we marched. The pit of my stomach felt like a tight coil of dread, but the longer I stood there and surveyed the scene, memory flashes dancing in my brain, the more I felt the coil relax, and I let it go. It was wonderful to go there. It was a soul retrieval exercise, collecting fragments of myself that I left behind many years before. I now understand that all experiences, good or bad, have their place in the bigger, perfect scheme of things.

It was the days when the milkman delivered the milk and you could leave money in the empty milk bottles and it wouldn't get stolen. Garbage removals were done by real men, who had to be fit to run alongside a truck, unlike the mechanical trucks we have now. There were no self-serve petrol stations, and bars closed at 6.00 p.m. Shopping bags were made from brown paper, and fish and chips were wrapped in newspaper. There were no fast food chains, and most Australian families lived on meals of meat and three vegetables each night. Obesity was rare. So much has changed in such a short time.

As my siblings were older than I was and most of them were in their teenage years, there was always the latest music playing. Bands such as the Beatles, Credence Clearwater Revival, and the Rolling Stones, musicians such as Elvis Presley, and all the latest sixties tunes were played regularly on the old-fashioned record player. When I reminisce about my childhood, I hear the music accompanying the memories.

The radio always seemed to be playing, and with so many children around, a good argument was always to be heard somewhere in the house. There was often an injury or an illness. I remember how it was commonplace then for the doctor to visit the house. He would arrive, always well-dressed, carrying his leather medical bag, and he had such a superior air about him. We all had to be on our best behaviour. We were certainly taught manners as children, at least to the outside world. However, when competing with many siblings, manners were the last thing on any of our minds, and cruel jabs and put downs were a big part of sibling communication.

My parents were Aussie battlers and worked hard. Their values were simple and typical of that era: girls grew up to marry and reproduce whilst boys grew up to work hard to provide an income.

I had a close relationship with my mother and still do. My Gemini mother has a happy-go-lucky disposition, and during our childhood she tended to take it all in her stride. Mum's slightly nervy disposition was often masked by her consistent smiling, chatting, and laughing. Mum always has a saying for any situation: 'We'll cross that bridge when we come to it', or 'You never know what's around the corner'. My mum is an attractive woman. I have a memory of her sitting at her old-fashioned dressing table letting her long, dark hair down at the end of the day. I would lie on her bed while she brushed her hair, applied her face cream, and chatted with me. My parents shared a room with single beds, which was not unusual in those days. Sometimes, on a Sunday morning, the only day Mum would not be up at the crack of dawn, I would jump into her sweet-scented bed. The sun would stream through the eastern window above her bed, and I delighted in watching the dust particles dance in the sunlight while feeling secure in her warm presence. My father in the adjacent bed would be snoring loudly, but at least in his sleep he was peaceful. Something as simple as that is actually one of my happiest childhood memories.

Mum was from a large family and was brought up on a dairy farm in South Australia. Always the optimist, practical and grounded, Mum was no stranger to hard work. Her parents were religious but loving souls, and Mum seemed to have inherited their warmth. Mum certainly had her work cut out for her. It was a huge task raising a large family while working part-time and persevering with a volatile marriage.

As loving and stable as Mum was, as a child I felt my needs paled in comparison to hers so often I wouldn't ask for what I needed. To me she seemed like this superwoman solving a million problems every minute. This pattern of putting my own needs aside is something I would have to work on later in life, and to some extent I still am. There is a lot more awareness now of the importance of expressing feelings and needs, but many of us still 'sit' on things in fear of upsetting others or not being loved. From my own experience I know this can be detrimental to our health. At the age of forty-five, I was confronted with throat cancer, a testament in my mind to 'sitting on things'. I came through that well in the end but wished I had confronted many issues earlier.

My Gemini dad, Arthur, worked hard. He loved his beer and cigarettes. I always felt quite emotionally distant from him. Being a parent myself now and feeling emotionally close to my own children, I can't imagine how it must feel for parents to feel disconnected from their own flesh and blood. It brings a sacred sort of joy to feel close to your child. Sadly, it was a common scenario for many fathers of that era. Many saw that as the mother's job, not the father's.

My father's routine was quite predictable. Each weeknight, Dad would arrive home from his after-work drinks and complain about whatever meal Mum had made, although he usually ate it anyway. After that he would settle down in the same spot at the kitchen table with his tall bottle of beer and Viscount cigarettes. The red and black cigarette packet sat beside a box of Redhead matches, the ones with the animated picture of a red-haired lady on the box. Accompanying the cigarettes would be an old-fashioned beer glass parked at its regular space. The amber bottle would be open, and the subtle smell of ale would line the air.

Sometimes when my father left the room, I picked up the cigarette box and smelled the strong tobacco scent and fingered the foil that encased the firmly packed white sticks. I would take one out and pretend it was lit and wonder what it would be like to be an adult. I am not sure to this day if it is normal behaviour for a child to fantasise about being an adult. I would often lie on my bed and imagine what I was going to look like, who my husband would be, where I would live, and how many children I would have. I would have wonderful clothes and do whatever I liked. Perhaps I did this as an escape from the unhappiness I felt in the home.

I assume having to feed a family of nine was a huge pressure, and I never remember Dad looking very happy except when he was tipsy. Then he would relax, crack jokes, and share his hearty laugh. However, if he drank too much he wasn't pleasant at all, and I felt like I had to walk on eggshells. We all did.

I recall peeking through the kitchen door's old-fashioned keyhole. Dad would be sitting at the long, oval-shaped kitchen table, his thin lips dragging on his cigarette, filling the room with smoke. His weathered hands raised his beer glass in celebratory mode to the record player. The music he would be singing along with was likely to be Frank Sinatra, Dean Martin, or Doris Day. After a track was complete, he would say, 'Beautiful, Doris, sing it again'. Then he would proceed to replay the same track over and over. My sister and I, hiding behind the door, would quickly place our hands over our mouths to prevent the rising giggles escaping and avoid being caught.

In his youth, my father had been a singer. He had even made a record that he had paid for, which came to an abrupt end when one of my brothers sat on the only copy he had.

Perhaps he had felt at that point in his life it had become an unfulfilled and impossible dream. I guess his way of dealing with it was drowning it in his beer glass, closing his eyes, and singing into his past.

Dad would sit there alone whilst we children would make ourselves scarce in fear of saying or doing something to upset him. Mum would be knitting in front of the television with her cup of tea nearby, always smiling, chatting, and laughing, putting up the front that all was well when you knew intuitively it wasn't.

This blatant dissonance was an ongoing, underlying feeling and theme right throughout my childhood that propelled me to seek and find something greater, something harmonious—in short . . . peace.

Two Gemini parents were challenging and they often argued. Saturday nights seemed to be the worst. There was many a Saturday night when Mum would throw us into the car to give Dad time to calm down. There were no seat belt laws then, so there would be arms and legs hanging out the windows while we all argued and jostled for the best position. We would often go to a drive-in movie up the road, which I didn't mind at all. It certainly beat staying at home listening to arguments. There was an insidious excitement about the whole situation that got my adrenaline pumping. Perhaps that is why as a teenager I was often a risk taker and searching for excitement. What we get used to as children becomes 'normal', even if it is dysfunctional or unhealthy.

Through my eyes as a child, I interpreted my father's disregard for me as not being good enough or worthy of attention. I didn't feel like he hated me. It felt more like I was ignored and didn't deserve any attention. A child's logic will assume there is something wrong with himself or herself. It makes sense to me that if a child does not have the security of knowing a parent loves them, there is a high chance he or she will suffer from self-esteem issues and feelings of unworthiness. I played out this need for approval through my relationships with men as an adult.

The local priest, Father Morris, would occasionally visit our house. I recall my mother fussing over him with a pot of steaming tea and homemade scones. I liked him; he seemed sincere and kind. He would sit at the kitchen table and pray for the family, particularly my father.

I still remember Father Morris's voice: 'Please, God, stop Arthur drinking'. *Wow*, I thought, *can God really do that?* This really piqued my curiosity. I found this interesting but strange and wondered how God was going to help or if he was really listening. Sitting at the kitchen table in his black robe and stiff white collar, Father Morris did look rather impressive. Perhaps he did have some power that normal people didn't to conjure up God. I was fully alert when he visited, half-hoping something magical might occur. It never did, and I always felt slightly disappointed when he left. I guess even then my higher self was waiting for the interesting, spiritual part of my life to reveal itself.

An underlying feeling throughout my childhood was that the external situation I found myself in didn't match the inner feelings I had. I felt a strong sense of joy for life, an excitement I felt in nature, and a knowing there was something so special about being alive. There seemed to be unhappiness and heaviness around me. Sometimes I see childhood visions in black and white, and that describes how I felt then. Huge pieces of something were missing.

Whenever I asked anyone where was God, the answer was always 'everywhere'. If he was everywhere, why couldn't I see or hear him?

However, that didn't stop me loving going to Sunday school. We attended the Baptist Church not far from home, and at one point my mother was a Sunday-school teacher. I recall the small white cottage across the road from the church where the classes were held. I skipped happily down the path past the pansies and daisies, wearing my clean, well-ironed hand-me-down. I loved going there because they told stories about this compassionate, lovely man called Jesus. He sounded wonderful and I idolised him. There was a small picture on the dusty bookcase in our lounge room of Jesus with a golden halo around his head. When I was feeling sad and no one was around, I used to stare at the picture and talk to him. I loved looking at that light around his head and figured only people in heaven must have that. Now I know we all have a light around our heads; we just can't see it.

What I didn't like about church were the services with the minister; they were so boring. I really didn't understand a word he said. Reading from the Bible has always sounded like a foreign language to me (it still does). I am sure the Bible holds some good thoughts in it; I just have never worked it out.

One day I was sitting up in front of the church, and all these people came onto the stage in white robes, and the minister began to dunk them in a bath of water. I assume now this was a ritual of the Baptist Church to cleanse them of their sins. As I was trying to fathom what was happening, my mother appeared on the stage. I became distressed, and someone had to take me out of the church. I thought they were going to drown her!

I am grateful the element of the church and Christianity was part of my childhood, as it was the only thing that indicated there may be more to life than meets the eye. It gave me a sense of hope.

There comes a point in life where one can really benefit from looking back at our childhood and seeing behavioural patterns we implemented then and how we carry them through into our adult lives. Once awareness is achieved, healing then begins. Awareness is light, and once it is bought out of the dark, it can't control us as it does when it sits in a hidden shadow.

Having said that, I also believe some patterns are so ingrained in our subconscious psyches they may never be completely removed but can be used to benefit rather than hinder us. It is no wonder psychology always interested me and that eventually I became a counsellor.

I am sure one of the lessons that my soul desired to learn before being born was independence. The family I was born into was the perfect vehicle. Being the youngest of seven, I had to learn to defend myself, and it made me independent from a young age. This independence has, at times, been my ally, but at other times my downfall. I have come to see that, sometimes, stubborn pride can be a by-product of independence and can isolate one from receiving love and support.

Childhood memories last a lifetime, and I am convinced that our early experiences, positive and negative, are part of a greater plan. Whatever observations and learning we take from our childhood somehow prepare us for what lies ahead. My childhood taught me humility, strength, compassion, and to endure being outside my comfort zone. It has also taken a lot of self-healing and mistakes to learn how to find the gems in these patterns and lessons.

There is a shadow side and a light side to all things, a yin and a yang, an opposite, a balance.

When I was younger, I used the humility I embraced in childhood to fuel low self-esteem. As an older and wiser person, I used it to keep me grounded and realise I was no more special than anyone else, even though I seemed to have an extraordinary gift.

I initially used the lessons of courage to make unwise choices, like running away to Sydney when I was twelve years old. I used it later to go outside my comfort zone, like learning to talk to dead people. I used the message of insidious excitement I received as a child to initially do some crazy things, like experiment with drugs. As I matured, it helped me to be adventurous and open to the unusual and to experiment with spiritual highs. The spiritual feelings activated through learning about Jesus, as a child, gave me a hope that there was something more to life that perhaps I could find.

No matter what sort of childhood you had, there were gems there even if they were disguised as gross injustices. Sometimes you have to search in the muck for a gem, but if you persevere you will find and embrace them. You will then know you have always had the tools to achieve whatever it was you came here for.

Then there are the incidents that come out of left field. These are the ones you never saw coming, which make life so very interesting and unpredictable. This is often how we get the 'knowing' that there is indeed more going on than meets the eye.

One such incident that went totally over my head happened at the tender age of four.

Chapter 2

The Undeveloped Medium

My first vivid memory of a psychic experience is when I was four years old visiting a friend of the family, whom we all called Uncle Jack. Jack and his wife were connected to the same church we attended. I remember Jack as a very warm and funny man. He had a stocky build and thick black hair, an infectious laugh, and a twinkle in his eye. He was popular amongst the children, as he was one of those rare adults of that era who understood that children liked to communicate with adults and have fun.

I remember arriving this particular day at Uncle Jack's white weatherboard home, which always symbolised to me a space that was warm and safe. The moment I saw Uncle Jack, I burst into tears. I kept hearing a voice in my head that repeated over and over, *You will never see Uncle Jack again*. When I was asked what was wrong and why I was crying, I replied, 'I am never going to see Uncle Jack again'. There was an awkward silence, and then I was told to be quiet and given a stern look by my father. I felt uncomfortable during the whole visit. I don't really recall much else about being four, but this experience is quite vivid. I now know I was having a clairaudient experience—that is, I was 'hearing' Spirit. Uncle Jack died suddenly that night of a heart attack, and of course we never saw him again. He was not that old and it was totally unexpected. I didn't understand why I had heard the voices and why no one else had.

The love of Spirit was at work one miserable, grey day in my younger years. I was six and sitting in the schoolyard on an empty bench watching the other children play. I had a bad habit of grabbing a piece of my hair and sucking it. It must have been some type of insecurity reflex. As I sat there in my grey linen skirt and my stiff white shirt sucking my hair, I wondered why I always seemed to be alone in the schoolyard. Children were laughing and playing together, and I felt totally left out. I so much wanted a friend, and for some reason no one ever approached me or wanted to play with me. Maybe it was my hand-me-down clothes, or maybe they sensed something different about me.

As I sat there feeling quite lonely, I clearly heard a velvety, warm female voice in my ear say, 'Do not worry, this is only for now, life will change, all things change'. After that I cheered up considerably. I intuitively knew the voice spoke the truth and that the discomfort I was feeling was temporary. I don't remember thinking it was strange that this voice talked to me. I thought perhaps everyone could hear these voices sometimes. It wasn't until I tried to tell a girl in my class about the voice and she gave me the most shocking look, as though I was a mad person, that I began to understand that maybe others didn't hear these things. Her reaction only served to confirm that perhaps I truly was a bit odd, which saddened me. Like most children, I just wanted to fit in.

Looking back, I realise the velvety voice I had heard in my ear that day belonged to one of my guardian angels. I have always found it easy to 'hear' Spirit. This is known as 'clairaudience', and it is not uncommon for us to be more natural with one psychic sense than another. When you experience clairaudience, it is usually hearing a voice in your head, not on the outside. One learns over time how to distinguish the voices from your own thoughts. I am sure many of you reading this have had similar experiences. The trick is to give these voices credit and be open to them before discounting them as nothing.

True to the angel's word, it was not long after that I made a wonderful friend, Carmen. Carmen was a kind, gentle, stunning-looking girl. She had long, straight black hair with brown, almond-shaped eyes, and a smile that lit up the room. I recently caught up with her after forty-odd years thanks to the magic of social networking. She is just as beautiful as she always was.

Carmen was like a light in my life at that time. I believe Spirit sends us angels in human form when we really need them. We loved being in each other's company, and I spent many hours playing at her house. The energy at her house felt much lighter than mine and in a way gave me some respite. Her older teenage sister, Doris, often burnt incense, which was the first time I had ever smelt it. I loved it. One fond memory is of Carmen and me dancing to the song 'The Age of Aquarius' while writing in the air with incense. As I waved around the black sticks, creating patterns with the swirling streams of scented smoke, a type of euphoria embraced my higher senses. The caged light inside me that was often filtered through a narrow passage of expected behaviour was beginning to awaken.

It was the late 1960s, and there was a sense of magic in the air. The world was on a roll. There were horrific things happening, such as the Vietnam War. Yet, running parallel was a new consciousness; a new wave of thinking was being born. Although we as children were blissfully unaware, the music and the mood of the planet were prevalent and the younger generation were strong and demanding.

Like the process of osmosis, we were taking it all in.

Doris and one of her high school friends made a Ouija board. These girls were much older than Carmen and me, so we thought they were wise and wonderful.

For those of you who are not familiar, a Ouija board is where you have the letters of the alphabet in a circle including the words 'yes' and 'no'. In the centre sits a glass placed upside down, usually a light wine glass. You then conduct a séance, which is where you call in spirits. The people present sit in a circle and place one finger on the glass and ask any spirits available to join the circle. You ask questions and the glass moves from letter to letter communicating with you. There is always the doubt present that someone is pushing the glass, and maybe someone is. Now, before I go any further, I want to say, please do not try this. Seriously, this is the wrong way to call in Spirit and you could attract undesirable energy. We were just kids experimenting, and I recall a few scary moments during those séances.

It felt mischievous and exciting gathering together to make the letters, select the right glass, and make sure no parents were around when we would have these sessions. It would take a while for us to settle down and go through the motions of accusing each other of pushing the glass. Then when we least expected it, the glass seemed to come alive and begin darting around while one of us would furiously write down the letters it was pointing to. It would spell out names, dates, or the way the spirit had died. The session usually ended when our fear levels reached our limit and we would all swear we would never do it again. Of course it would not be long until our curiosity and desire for excitement would take over.

During one session, the glass literally jumped up and broke. Perhaps it was an unhappy spirit or perhaps it was one our guides trying to discourage us. Upon reflection, it is possible those days had a profound effect on me. The problem with Ouija boards is that they can attract earthbound spirits. Sometimes these spirits are mischievous and can impersonate other people. For example, the Ouija board might tell you it is your grandmother who has passed on, but actually it is some lost soul. If you want to contact someone who has passed, the best way is to contact a reputable medium. I guess one day we became scared and stopped using the Ouija board or perhaps we just grew out of it, but it was one of those memories that never went away.

When I was eleven years old we moved house. It was a huge change for the whole family, and we found ourselves downsizing to a smaller, newly built home. It also meant I had to change schools. I was so sad to leave the only home I had ever known. I loved that place. However, besides my friendship with Carmen, I was really unhappy at the school I attended. I had a teacher from hell that was so strict, she scared the life out of me, and every day was a nightmare. With mixed feelings and no choice in the matter, life moved on, as it does.

The new school proved to be wonderful and modern, with young, switched-on teachers. For the first time in my life I quickly became one of the popular kids. It was such a drastic change, and one my soul needed badly at the time. Things at home were still not great, and my parents were going through their own changes now that their youngest was almost in high school, and some of the older children were leaving home and getting married.

The next psychic experience I remember was when I was eleven years old and having a very vivid dream that the caretaker at my new school died. In my dream, everything was in slow motion but vivid and clear. I was outside the school building and the caretaker came up to me and said in a slow, deep, and haunting voice, 'I am dead'. The next morning we had an assembly at school to announce that the caretaker had passed away in the night. I was flabbergasted. I wanted to share it with someone but knew no one would believe me so I kept it to myself. It was then that I began to wonder what was going on. Was something wrong with me?

There are many undeveloped mediums; perhaps you are one. It is clear to me now that the reason I was having these random psychic and medium experiences as I was growing up was because I was an undeveloped medium. Much like a pressure cooker, the energy sits within, dormant. Occasionally a bit of it escapes. Once a medium is trained and learns how to handle and harness the energy, these random experiences are less common.

If you find you have these random experiences such as visitations from the other side, it is likely you are an undeveloped medium. If it does bother you, you have a few choices. Either you learn to develop your gifts and become a practising medium, or you need to learn enough to know how to put a 'lid' on it and develop confidence handling it. A good, reputable medium should be able to help you. There is a saying: 'When the student is ready, the teacher appears', and I believe that is true. Ask Spirit for your teacher to appear, and I have no doubt that something will happen if you ask from a point of complete sincerity. I believe that is a hidden law of the universe.

In my early teens, the very first book that had a spiritual influence on me was *The Third Eye* by Lobsang Rampa. Some of my older readers may remember the author, Lobsang Rampa. *The Third Eye* was supposedly an autobiography. (I am not sure if it was true, but it illustrated spiritual ideas and philosophies along Buddhist lines.) I was fascinated and read every book by the author I could get hold of. I went on to have normal teenage experiences, such as my first kiss and attending my first rock concert.

Yet while doing all these so-called 'normal' things, like many of us, deep inside I felt anything but normal. I was restless and longing to explore what life was all about. In high school I felt like a fish out of water. I was older "in my head" than the other kids, and my report cards mentioned I was a bright and mature student. I would often spend time in the schoolyard talking to the teachers on duty. I was lonely and prayed to whoever might be listening to send me a friend. Then one magical day I arrived at school and ran straight into a 'new' girl. Debbie was a tall, blonde earth angel with a wicked sense of humour and felt as 'odd' as I did. We were inseparable and had so much fun although we were not always 'good'. Spirit had answered my lonely prayers once again.

By the time I was almost fourteen, my mother found the courage to leave my father. They hadn't been happy for many years, and now that most of the children had left home, the time was ripe. The only way she knew how to do it was to slip out quietly without a drama and then communicate through lawyers, which is exactly what happened. That was the day that is etched in my memory, the day we left when Dad was at work.

As a teenager in the 1970s, I experimented with drugs, and the experiences I had while under the influence of LSD only confirmed to me there were other realms of existence and that the soul was so much deeper than we could fathom.

I left school at fifteen and had several jobs. Although I had the academic potential to do well by furthering my education, I was far too restless to continue school at that point. My mother was remarrying, and although she welcomed me to stay with her, I wanted to have my independence and own income. I started a hairdressing apprenticeship that lasted six months. The day I used conditioner instead of shampoo on a rich client's hair was the end of my hairdressing career. I worked in a university bookshop, as a receptionist in an office, and as a packer in a warehouse. There seemed to be plenty of jobs for bright fifteen-year-olds at that time. I kept changing jobs in a desperate desire to find whatever it was I was looking for, and I had no idea what that was. I was dissatisfied, and there was an underlying urgency to keep searching.

What I didn't know at that point was that Spirit did have a plan for me and that my spiritual world was just about to open up.

Chapter 3

There Is a Plan

My spiritual path began to evolve in 1977, when I was sixteen. My girlfriend Rita and I worked hard to save some money to go travelling around Australia. We met when working at a large, breezy cosmetic warehouse in St. Kilda. We started chatting whilst packing mascaras and lipsticks. We clicked straightaway. One morning over a cup of coffee, Rita said, 'I really want to travel around Australia but I have no one to do it with'.

'You're kidding!' I said, 'Me too!' I had recently broken up with my first love and had a strong desire for new experiences. Always searching, I had already started saving to travel without any real plan. Of course having a friend to travel with was the best plan.

Rita was a lovely girl with a big heart. She was tall with raven-black hair, huge brown eyes, and olive skin. We had big dreams and simply couldn't wait to get going. We bought large canvas backpacks and thought we were so very cool. Rita's mother insisted we stop at a country town in New South Wales to check in with some of her friends who lived there to make sure we were okay. Rita told me she had met her mum's friend, Will, several times when he had visited Melbourne and assured me that I would love him.

Rita's mum drove us to the Hume Highway and had made us cheese and alfalfa sandwiches for lunch, which we ate by the side of the road. It was a glorious sunlit day, and the sound of the trucks and traffic whizzing by added to the anticipation and excitement we were feeling. Rita's mum read us the riot act about staying safe before she let us go. In those days there wasn't as much fear around hitchhiking, although in hindsight I know now we were taking a risk. My mind drifted back to the last time I was standing there on the Hume Highway a few years earlier when I ran away. This time was different; I was older, had my own money, and felt free to make my own decisions. At sixteen I thought I was invincible!

Our stomachs full and unable to wait another minute, we said goodbye and began hitchhiking. It took a few lifts and an overnight stay to get to our destination. Luckily it was without any major incidents.

Sitting up high in the cab of a huge transport truck with Rita's head nodding off on my shoulder, the burly truck driver announced, 'Here we go, girls, this is where you get off'. We had arrived at our destination, inland New South Wales, on a hot and dry summer afternoon.

The sun was high and our backpacks were heavy as we made our way down some wide, tree-lined streets following the map Rita's mum had provided. We walked on cracked, dry mud as we cut through a park, noticing that the yellow grass and thirsty-looking eucalypts were crying out for rain. I'd wished I'd packed some insect repellent as the blowflies buzzed around our ears.

The air, thick with heat, blew gentle summer scents that were different from Melbourne. My senses were absorbing the foreign atmosphere. Magpies cried and kookaburras laughed as we passed some large pine trees. Rita and I chatted excitedly and giggled as teenage girls do. As we left the park behind us and entered the streets again, I noticed the houses were old, original-looking country homes.

We came to the address we were looking for and found a blue weatherboard house half-covered in a flowering vine, framed by an overgrown garden, and a white letterbox that was half-broken. As we approached the front door and the shady porch, we could smell incense burning and hear the faint sound of music playing. I smiled as I realised it was one of my favourite bands, The Moody Blues.

Three black and white cats lying on an old couch on the porch eyed us suspiciously as we twisted the small lever that rang the doorbell. Within seconds the door swung wide open. In front of us stood a stocky gentleman in his early thirties, brown hair to his shoulders, a rough beard to match, and the widest, most genuine smile we had seen for the last couple of days on the road. Rita embraced him warmly and introduced me to Will. He then put his arm around both of us and led us into a messy but welcoming kitchen. He put the kettle on and asked us to tell him about all of our adventures. Although we didn't know it at that point, Will was to become our surrogate dad for the next six months.

'So do you girls believe in life after death?' Will asked, surprising us halfway through the fresh cup of Earl Grey tea he had just brewed us.

Rita and I looked at each other not knowing what to say and started giggling again.

'You know, it's good to be open-minded about other realms of existence. Just because you can't see them doesn't mean they aren't there', Will said.

'Do you mean aliens as well?' Rita asked, her big brown eyes looking extra wide and bright.

'Maybe; anything is possible, Rita', Will said. 'What do you think, Liz?'

I looked into Will's kind eyes and felt shy and unsure of what to say. 'I think there is something, but I am not sure what', I mumbled.

Will said quite ominously, 'Well, ladies, if you are not in a hurry, hang around here for a while and you might be in for a few surprises'.

Rita and I looked at each other and giggled again, and in the pit of my stomach where intuition lives, I felt a rush of good feeling.

Will continued to drop meaningful things into his conversation. Then he would stop talking and look at us, waiting for us to ask him for an explanation. Something deep inside me that had been asleep for a long time began to awaken. I began to get an idea that something was going on here, something spiritual. What really excited me was not so much what Will was talking about rather how happy and peaceful he seemed in himself. It showed in his eyes, and the eyes do not lie; they truly are the mirrors of the soul. To be honest, I wasn't completely sure what he was talking about. I racked my memory from the Lobsang Rampa books I had read, my only frame of reference at the time, but I felt quite out of my depth. Will talked about astral planes and Spirit Guides, and I felt a thirst inside me wanting to know more.

The mystery unfolded more clearly in the next few days as we started to meet Will's friends. Will was involved in a psychic development group. This was a totally unexpected turn of events. I am not sure now how much Rita knew about this beforehand, but she certainly had never mentioned any of the psychic connections to me. Here was a plan unfolding once again.

There would have been about thirty people from the local community involved. Will's house seemed to be the hub of activity where people would drop in for a cup of tea and a chat, so it didn't take long to get to know everyone. They didn't drink or do drugs and they were relaxed and open-minded people. The Moody Blues music always seemed to be playing, and to this day that band reminds me of my time there. They would plan simple but fun events, like getting up at 4.00 a.m. and driving to a mountain to see the sunrise while we had a barbecue breakfast. They were lovely people who took us under their wings. I learnt to cook my first vegetarian meal as well as how to meditate. Will kept an eye out for us and was always there to talk about anything we needed help with. Before we knew it, months had gone by and our backpacks acquired dust. We were having such a wonderful time, all thoughts of travelling had been forgotten.

Rita and I were invited to attend a psychic development class twice a week. We learnt about visualisation, manifestation techniques, brainwaves, meditation, Spirit Guides, working with our breath, and even numerology and how to use it.

I felt nervous about attending the first class and didn't know what to expect, but at the same time I couldn't wait to get there. It was held in a small community hall, and when we arrived I noticed a few familiar faces and I began to relax. There must have been about twenty of us in one room and twenty in another. Our teachers were a married couple, Jana and Pete, who were kind and easy going.

The class began and you could hear a pin drop. I felt like I was holding my breath. Within minutes Pete and Jana had us laughing and loosening up. There was a focus on visualisation techniques, which improved memory and clairvoyance. I felt like Alice in Wonderland and was amazed there was an option to actually develop hidden skills like this. We learnt about different brain waves—alpha, beta, and delta—and how to reach these states, use them to find peace, and visualise success.

The first night, we were asked to close our eyes and relax. Then we were asked to visualise a large golden ball of light in the centre of our foreheads. As our focus became distracted, we were guided to keep bringing the focus back to the golden ball of light. I found it difficult, and my mind was wandering all over the place. I improved over time, and we were reassured it is normal to have a short attention span. I had just learnt my first meditation. I realise now that this exercise was to open the third eye chakra centre, which is one of the keys to seeing clairvoyantly.

Our homework one week was to practise the art of the law of attraction. The idea was to think of a small solid object that you would like to own. The next step was to keep visualising it in as much detail as you could and keep seeing yourself with the object. Pete stressed to start small and work your way up. I chose an incense holder because I thought that would be small enough. Each day I would practice seeing the golden ball of light during my meditation, and then I would do my homework. I would visualise a small, round, colourfully beaded incense holder. I would imagine holding it and feeling its texture. I would see myself placing the incense in it and lighting it.

A week later, one morning I was sitting on a bench in the park reading a book about astrology that I had borrowed from Will. Amber rays of the sun warmed my face and children played nearby. I was totally immersed in my book when I felt a tugging on my skirt. I prised myself away from the page and found a small face circled with blond hair and bright blue eyes looking straight into mine.

'Excuse me, Miss', the owner of the small face said. 'Is this yours?' The little boy who stood before me must have been no older than six years. In his open hand sat a small, round, beaded incense holder. It was an exact replica of the one I had been trying to manifest, and here it was, in the physical, looking at me.

I opened my mouth to speak and hesitated as I registered what was happening and felt an excitement within me begin to rise. 'Well no, it isn't mine. Where did you find it?'

'Under the seat', he pointed.

I was about to reply when he simply shoved it in my hand and ran off, eager to get back to his play. I put the book down and sat and stared at this small object as if it was the most miraculous thing I had ever seen. To be delivered straight into my hands like that was amazing. How it got to be under the bench I was sitting on I will never know. I also question what drew me to go to the park that day and to sit on that particular seat. Perhaps it was the law of attraction. I couldn't wait to get home to tell Rita and Will.

When I arrived at the next class, it seemed others had also had some success stories. One girl had ignored the advice about starting small because she was in desperate need of a car. Within a few days of her doing her homework she was offered a car for free. The problem was it was an old bomb that needed work and was unregistered. Pete explained this is why it is so important to be precise and to visualise the details. The girl had put out for a car but not necessarily a car that worked. Another student had manifested free tickets to a concert, which were then given to him by a relative. These successes were inspiring, but more than anything it was changing the way I thought and was opening me up to a whole new world. Over the years I have learnt that one of the most important ingredients to manifesting is using feeling and emotion. For example, the girl who needed the car could have focused on how good it would feel to have the car and how satisfied she would have felt.

There was no real name for the group; it just was what it was. The focus was on self-development rather than giving readings to other people.

My time there was magical and uplifting. It felt like a new door opening in my life that hinted at limitless possibilities. It was my first conscious introduction to an inner world that had always been there that I didn't know existed, even though I sort of did.

Like looking through a kaleidoscope for the first time, I was in awe. Learning to turn my vibrant sixteen-year-old senses inward had a powerful impact on me and my perceptions. It felt like the hand of fate had placed me there for a reason.

I became friendly with a young man in the class, Chris. Chris was a tall, slim guy with a mop of frizzy dark hair. I didn't know much about him except that he was also from Melbourne and a traveller. After class a few of us would often go out for a coffee, and this was how I connected with Chris. He had a certain peaceful aura about him and seemed old and wise to me at the time, but I think he would have been all of nineteen or twenty. We had an easy-going connection, and although there was some romance, it felt more like friendship. He asked me to travel with him to Queensland for a week or two. Having never seen Queensland, I jumped at the opportunity.

We had a great time on the road. We stopped in beautiful Byron Bay and breathed in the wonder and beauty of the northeast coast. We slept on the beach under the stars, which was a first for me. As I listened to the crash of the ocean while watching the frilly outline of the moonlit waves, I felt a deep longing to find a place of peace within me. I was roughing it and loving it. We lived on fruit, bread, and vegemite and the odd takeaway. We checked out the glitzy Gold Coast and the sprawling city of Brisbane.

All was going well until one evening we were camping north of Brisbane in a tiny coastal town called Tin Can Bay. Chris had a steel-framed pyramid that was easily dismantled, so every night he would set up the pyramid and we would sleep in the tent under it. It was an 'in' thing then to have a steel-framed pyramid if you were into spirituality, and an alternative bookshop in Melbourne sold them. Apparently, by meditating or sleeping under them, your energy was raised and you could achieve a higher state of consciousness. We must have looked a funny sight for passers-by, all tucked into bed under the pyramid.

This particular evening the pyramid may well have worked its magic, as I had a vivid dream of a beautiful, heavenly woman who gave me specific instructions. She appeared in a shimmering array of golden light. I am aware now that this beautiful woman was one of my guardian angels, but in the 1970s we weren't up to angels yet. This woman told me that when I woke in the morning, I must go straight to the local train station and return to the country town where Rita and Will were. She said, 'Chris will try to stop you, but this is important; just go!' There was a strong sense of urgency in the dream, so I knew I had to do what I was told. I didn't really want to leave, as I was having a good time, but nevertheless I did.

Chris certainly did try to stop me and chased me all the way to the train station. When he saw how determined I was he surrendered, and we said a tearful goodbye. I am not sure why, but I didn't tell him about my dream.

I arrived back the next day feeling flat and fell sobbing into Rita's arms. I wondered what had just happened. As is often the case, there was a bigger picture I couldn't see at the time but obviously Spirit could.

Chris turned up about three weeks later with a tale to tell.

After I had left he continued on his travels north and decided to stop for a walk in a state forest. Chris lost his bearings and was lost in the forest for three days with no food, water, or shelter. Eventually he found his way out, hungry, dazed, and confused. If I had not listened to the dream, I would have gone through all that with him. Obviously my Spirit helpers wanted to protect me. I felt so relieved I had been spared. It was a good lesson in acknowledging dreams and trusting intuition.

Chris went back to Melbourne, and whatever we had together ceased to be. I did catch up with him a few years later for a coffee, and we had a laugh about the whole affair. I lost contact with him after that.

The months flew by and summer turned to autumn. We were feeling very comfortable in our new lives at Will's house, and every day I was learning something. Whether it was about meditation, astrology, or cooking, I was loving life. However, my savings were dwindling and there didn't seem to be much work around. I was getting a strong intuitive message that I should return to school, although I was totally resisting the idea. I often felt out of my depth in conversations and instinctively knew that furthering my education would boost my self-confidence. I also had a desire to be a nurse at that time and needed to complete high school to do so.

After we had been living there about six months, the gentleman who was the founder of the psychic group, Jim, turned up at Will's house. It was a little unusual for him to do house calls—most people went to see him if they needed him for something. I was surprised when he said he wanted to talk to me in private. My first thought was perhaps I had done something wrong or I was in trouble. He was respected within the psychic community, and I felt shy around him.

It was a cool, still, winter day as we sat outside next to a large lemon tree just as the sun made a timely appearance. I was so nervous I couldn't look him in the eyes and focused instead on some golden autumn leaves under his chair. Very gently, Jim told me that it was time for me to leave the community. He told me he had seen clairvoyantly that I had a big future ahead of me and my path was set to work with Spirit. He warned me that I had to be patient, though, as I had a bit to get through first. Spirit had suggested that I was to go back to Melbourne and return to school. He said it wouldn't be easy, but it was what I needed at that time. My gaze shifted from the leaves to Jim's eyes as my own eyes now filled with tears. I had no words to say or arguments to give. His eyes looked back at me full of compassion and understanding, and without any more words, he simply hugged me until my sobs subsided.

Somewhere inside I had been intuitively getting a similar message but had been ignoring it. Jim whispered, 'It's all going to work out; you will be looked after'. At that moment, a Willy Wagtail sat on the lemon tree branch that was closest to us and started singing its song. It was the perfect moment that broke the tension and we both laughed.

'What about Rita?' I asked him.

'Her fate lies here', Jim said.

I didn't want to go but felt I had no choice. I totally trusted Jim's words and had no doubt he had received his information from a higher source. I felt sad, as I had always felt socially awkward, and now I had finally found somewhere I thought I belonged, but Spirit had other ideas. Out of respect for the community and my own intuition, I felt it was the right thing to do.

Out came the backpack and off I went. Rita and Will drove me to the train station. It seemed apt it was an icy cold evening and fog was setting in. As we arrived, I was relieved that the loudspeaker was asking passengers travelling to Melbourne to immediately board the train. I hate goodbyes and was already feeling emotional. I gave them both quick but warm hugs and thanked them both.

Will said, 'You are going to be fine. Remember, you are never alone'.

Rita whispered in my ear, 'I am really going to miss you'.

'And I you', I replied.

I still remember their encouraging faces, with just a hint of tears in Rita's eyes as the train pulled away. I held back my own tears and put on a brave face until they were out of sight and all I could hear was the loud rattle of the train. Looking around the empty carriage, I looked out the window to the night only to see my reflection and a sad face. I knew then it was okay to cry, and I did, on and off until I arrived back in Melbourne.

Inside myself now, in the present moment, I want to go back to my sixteen-year-old self and hug her and tell her how brave she was doing all that alone.

Rita stayed on there, and over the years we lost contact, so I am not really sure what happened to her. It was the last time I ever saw Rita and Will. I will always be grateful to them for being there at that time. It was time for a new chapter in my life.

Chapter 4

Down to Earth

J im was right!

It wasn't easy, and after having so much freedom and excitement it was hard for me to knuckle down and adjust to school life again. I was coming down to earth with a thud. It was complicated by the fact that I couldn't live at home, as my mother had remarried and was temporarily living in a caravan. My father had also remarried, and it wasn't an option to live with him. After a few months of staying with family, I knew it was time to find my own place, but I had no idea where to begin.

Out of the blue I met Emma, a girl who caught the same school bus as me. Emma asked me whether I knew anyone who was interested in sharing a house with her and a few others. I immediately let her know I was interested. Emma was warm and friendly, and we clicked straight away. Once again the universe had provided me with just what I needed then and there. We found a house and moved in. I made new friends, transferred to a nearby high school that I loved, and starting enjoying myself.

Embracing my new independence in the share house, I decided to visit the Laundromat. I set out one morning feeling bright and bubbly and began my journey down the main street. Halfway there, I left my body. It was totally random. Just like that, for about ten seconds I was above my body looking down at the top of my head and watching my body walk. I felt big, limitless, and was wondering how my body was walking without me in it. It scared and exhilarated me all at once. I felt so light in that short amount of time. It was amazing and I felt high for days afterward. In those ten seconds I realised I was not just my body. There was something else that had no limitations, no barriers, and I felt so free!

When I have read accounts of near-death experiences, the word 'free' is often used to describe the moment of passing over. If it is anything at all like those ten seconds, I totally understand. Although it was such a brief experience, it changed me. I now knew for sure, first hand, that there was a soul or a spirit within. I never told anyone at the time about this experience, as I didn't really know what had happened or how to explain it. Now I know so much more, I understand that I had classic symptoms of an undeveloped medium. Perhaps Spirit was trying to get my attention by confirming my suspicions that there was more to life than I understood.

The share house I lived in with three other girls was located in an inner city suburb. It was a cute, white weatherboard house in a bushy tree-lined street. Each of us had our own unique personalities, and it was an interesting household. Briana was the creative one, Emma was the party girl, and Rebecca was the sensible one—while I was the spiritual influence in the mix.

The scent of sea grass matting throughout the house reminded me of a balmy, woody forest. My bedroom was flooded by the sweet scent of the jasmine vine outside. I liked my spacious room and kept it neat. I loved to burn incense, light candles, and meditate using the techniques I had learnt in my psychic group.

Behind our house was a huge housing commission accommodation complex that was many stories high. It towered over our house and felt like an uninvited guest peeking into our backyard. It was tall, bleak, and grey and served to remind us that a real world lingered outside the cocoon we were living in. We had no idea at the time that someone in that building was watching us.

One evening, I returned home and noticed the back gate was open, which we never used. I casually mentioned it to my housemates, but none of us thought anything more about it. I realised the gate was open because our only toilet was an outhouse down next to the back gate, which I had just visited. Naive and unconcerned, we went to bed.

When I walked into my bedroom to go to sleep that evening, there was such a spiritual, high presence in the room you could have cut the air with a knife. The room was almost glowing, and I felt incredibly happy just being in the room. From my limited understanding I knew there were some higher energies visiting. It felt amazing and I didn't really understand why. I drifted off into a peaceful sleep.

In the middle of the night, I woke to a high-pitched scream coupled with loud footsteps heading out the front door. I jumped out of bed and flew to the light switch. Sleepily, I kept flicking the switch on and off with no result until I realised there was no power. Running through the house in the dark I found Emma in her room screaming, 'There was a man in my bed!'

Brianna's boyfriend, Joe, had stayed the night and reacted quickly and took flight down the street chasing a dark figure that merged into the night. Feeling shaky and rattled, we found some candles and everyone searched their rooms. The brazen intruder had cut the power and phone lines, entered bedrooms, and had even crept up to bedside tables and removed money and jewellery. He ended his tour of the house by popping into Emma's bed, but when she screamed he ran. It was a piercing scream that would have scared anyone!

The intruder had not even entered my room—the *only* room he didn't enter. Why? My intuition told me that was why I felt such a spiritual presence in my room earlier that evening. I intuitively knew I had been protected. This was before I knew about spiritual protection—they didn't teach me that at psychic school. I now assume Spirit thought it was okay to go ahead and protect me. Once again I was looked after. I felt sick when I realised that when I had gone to the toilet before bed, it was quite likely this anonymous figure was hiding in the backyard.

Although the thief was never caught, we heard rumours in the neighbourhood that it was someone living in the housing commission flats behind us. That awful feeling of having your safe space invaded prevailed for quite a while—we all slept huddled together in one bed with a cricket bat for months.

I believe that spiritual protection is the number one basic requirement for doing any psychic work. I was lucky in those days, as obviously Spirit had my back, but I don't take that for granted now. I always stress to my students again and again to make it a routine to protect yourself before opening up psychically. We are all like walking sponges whether we are aware of it or not, soaking up vibrations wherever we go. This is why it is so important where we put our focus. If we are around a lot of sadness, we can't help but take on some of that sadness. If we are around nature and beauty, the chances are you will absorb that energy.

Sometimes you can't avoid uncomfortable energy. For example, it may be your workplace or a social situation where you can't control the atmosphere, not completely anyway. The power we do have is to consistently clear old energy and protect ourselves, preferably daily.

This can be simple. You can use prayer or ask your angels and guides to do it for you. You can also have a salt bath, as salt absorbs negative energy, and you can follow up the bath with visualising yourself in a bright pink bubble of protection. You can use Native American sage sticks to clear energy around your body or home and then follow up with wearing a cleansed amethyst crystal for protection.

To protect a space, I like to visualise angels surrounding the property and each entry point. I pray to Archangel Michael to watch over the space with his beautiful sword of truth. When the energy is low, I surround the outside of the property with salt. Placing small bowls of water and salt in the corner of a home or office space will absorb any negative energy. Burning eucalyptus, lavender, or citrus oils is also cleansing and uplifting. Prayer is a powerful tool and can never be underestimated. Prayer combined with some of the methods I have mentioned will elevate the energy to an even higher level.

There are many ways to protect yourself, and I suggest you research and experiment with whatever makes you feel safe. If you feel safe, you are. Spiritual protection is like practising your scales when you are learning an instrument. It requires discipline and practice, but it pays off in the end.

The main objective with spiritual protection is to heighten the energy. When vibrations reach a certain frequency, lower vibrations cannot share the same space.

What I needed at that time in my life was some direction and guidance on what to do with the consistent voices I heard and the presences I often felt. I knew I was more than my body. I had learned that there was a spiritual power within, but I felt like I was missing some important pieces of a puzzle and had no idea where to look. Perhaps inside me I was asking for help because the next stage of my life led me to some of my most influential teachers. As the saying goes, 'When the student is ready, the teacher appears'.

Chapter 5

Mentors

My first direct experience with a medium was in 1978. A friend had told me of an amazing woman who was working from a spiritualist church in Melbourne. I rang to make an appointment and was told I would have to wait four weeks. I was disappointed, but the secretary explained that the medium was booked with back-to-back appointments. The big day finally arrived, and I recall being incredibly nervous. I'd had readings using numerology and tarot cards but never had I met a medium, let alone had a reading with one.

The reading was conducted in an old hall at the end of the inner city down a narrow street. As I hopped off the tram, littered papers danced around my feet that mirrored the jumpy feelings in my stomach. The metallic scent of traffic and industry invaded my nostrils. I pulled my long black coat close around me and tightened my scarf, partly because the cool wind was going through my whole body and partly because I was nervous.

When I found the building, the only indication it was the right one was a small, broken sign. I entered the building and found an elderly lady sitting at an old wooden desk. She kindly told me it wouldn't be long and to sit in the waiting area. As I took a seat, I was aware my stomach was full of butterflies, so to distract myself I began to take in my surroundings. An old-fashioned radiator gave the illusion of warmth, but the large building was full of drafts. Above were high ceilings, and I noticed an old wooden stairway leading up to another hall, which was apparently where Sunday spiritual services were held. There was a small printed sign on the wall saying 'Quiet, Please, Readings in Progress'. I could hear muffled voices and an occasional laugh coming through some of the thin walls.

It seemed that a number of small rooms had been created by using thin partition walls, and this is where the readings were taking place. There was a picture of Queen Elizabeth II hanging slightly crookedly on the wall, and I had to stop myself in my nervous state from hopping up and straightening it.

When I was eventually called into the room, my palms were sweating. I was so worried this woman would tell me awful things were going to happen to me, but at the same time I was intrigued.

I entered a small, dark room, and there was just enough light to make out an older lady sitting with her eyes closed. I was directed to sit on a rickety wooden chair.

The lady didn't even look at me. All she said was, 'Hello, dear, I'm Helen. Give me a moment and I will be with you'. Then she sat with her eyes closed, completely silent for what seemed a very long minute or two.

Without warning she started talking very quickly. There was so much information it was hard to take it all in. Within minutes I was absolutely startled when she mentioned Uncle Jack and how he had passed with a heart attack and that he sent his love.

Helen told me I would live for many years surrounded by greenery and trees. She also said I had a lot of psychic talent but I had no idea that I did and in time it would all make sense to me. Eventually, she told me, I would marry and have a son and that I mustn't worry about the future and that it would take care of itself. What seemed like five minutes later, there was a knock on the door indicating the half hour was up, and quite abruptly the reading ended. Without opening her eyes, Helen informed me that the session was finished and I must leave. I was in a stunned state. I paid the small fee and walked out of the dark hall squinting into the midday winter sunshine.

I felt exhilarated and my mind was racing. Flashes of Uncle Jack from when I was a child, flashes of everything I had learned when I stayed with Will, together with thoughts of what all this meant collided in my mind. This was confirmation of the afterlife I had not expected. On some deep level I knew what had just happened was true. It was like my soul breathed a sigh of relief.

I found it rather strange that this lady never opened her eyes to look at me once. I walked away feeling elated and strangely comforted. From that day on I was a total convert. I now believed for sure that Spirit existed and life went on after the grave. Eventually, everything Helen had said that day came true.

If any of you have had an evidential experience with a medium, you will know how it can change your whole perspective on life. If you haven't had this experience I highly recommend it. Ask Spirit to send the perfect medium for you and you may be surprised.

I visited Helen a few times in the coming years and always came away in awe and with a sense of comfort. Still, she never opened her eyes, so I felt she didn't know me.

It was not long after my reading with Helen that I started to feel a real emptiness inside me for no real reason that I could pinpoint. Inside, I felt like a flower that desperately needed water but had no idea where the source of water was. I had just turned seventeen, finished the school year, and I had a boyfriend, Michael, who was ten years older than I was. Besides there being some disapproval from both of our families about our age difference, there was nothing really particularly wrong, but I found myself crying and not knowing why. I was unsure at this stage what I was to do next in my life on a work or study level, but I wasn't particularly worried about that. There was a strong desire to search for deeper meaning. I would spend hours in the theosophical bookshop, which was one of the only bookstores that stocked spiritual books back then.

Michael liked to read the tarot cards and was good at it. I would sit back and watch as he read for our friends and notice how they would get emotional as the cards would hit a raw nerve. I practised numerology that I had learnt in my psychic classes, which also seemed uncannily accurate. I started reading about spiritual teachers and gurus. One particular book I read said you don't choose a teacher, a teacher chooses you, and when the student is ready the teacher will appear. There and then I closed the book and prayed from the bottom of my heart, 'Please, if I have a teacher who has answers for me, please come into my life, please!' At that point I felt so desperate for truth and wanted to know what life was about. The prayer was directly from my heart. Was my life path just to grow up, work, marry, have children and die? There had to be more and I had to know. I knew I was more than my body by the experiences I'd had. There was a still a huge piece of the puzzle missing, and my heart ached for the truth.

That night I had a dream that a short man with a glowing face, who looked slightly Asian, was in a kitchen cooking with me. He said, 'Don't worry, it will be okay'. Then it felt like my whole being was swirling in a rainbow of light and colour. I woke up the next morning and felt fantastically altered and on a natural high. I had absolutely no doubt that something good was going to happen. Once again my dreams had been a guiding light. I told my boyfriend, Michael, and he asked me to describe the man in my dream. When I did, Michael mumbled something like 'Oh no, it's him; he is going to get me'.

'What are you talking about?" I asked, but he wouldn't elaborate.

The feeling of the dream sat with me, as sometimes special dreams do. I had a strong gut feeling there was more to come from it.

A week later I was visiting Michael's house and noticed a pamphlet tossed carelessly on a desk. I was drawn to pick it up and the photo on the pamphlet alarmed me. 'Oh my God, it's him!' I started shouting and jumping up and down. 'The man in my dream, it's him!'

Michael calmly replied, 'Mmm, thought so'.

The pamphlet said this man could show you inner peace. I wanted that! Michael then promised he would take me in the near future to a meeting that would explain more about this man, but he had his reasons why he didn't want to go to a Melbourne meeting. We were planning to travel soon, so I reluctantly agreed to wait. I am not sure why I didn't just go on my own; perhaps I felt overwhelmed by what had happened. I was absolutely blown away. I had asked from the bottom of my heart to be sent a teacher, and voila, here he was! It was a good lesson in praying from the heart that would come in handy many times in my future. I know now when you are stuck in life and you have no answers, there is only one thing to do. Hit the floor, be humble, and give the problem to a higher power. Own that you can't deal with it. Every time I have done that and meant it from the bottom of my heart, help has always arrived in some form; even it wasn't the way I expected it.

Michael soon confessed. He explained that his former girlfriend had become involved in this group and his relationship with her had ended. He blamed the guru for the separation, yet at the same time had been drawn to him. He had chosen to put it in the 'too hard' basket and get on with his life, and then he had met me. When I told him about my dream he knew it was the same guru from my description.

A few weeks later in early 1979, there was an advertisement in the paper for super cheap flights to Tasmania. We were keen to do some travelling but short on cash, so this seemed like a great opportunity. We packed our backpacks and headed for the airport. When we arrived it was explained to us that it was a standby situation. What ended up happening was that Michael left on one plane and I left on another. It was to be an omen for the near future.

Tasmania is an amazing place. Its emerald-green countryside coupled with its crisp fresh oceans seemed to awaken my sleeping cells within. I was bathing in the freedom from the smog of Melbourne. There I could think, I could breathe.

Once we arrived, we began hitchhiking and ended up camping on a remote beach, Coles Bay. It then occurred to us that the weekend was approaching and we had no cash. Michael left me on the beach to find a bank but returned that evening empty-handed. He couldn't find one nearby, so we were forced to fast without food for the next few days. It was a huge detox that we had to surrender to. However, it was a beautiful beach, and I spent hours staring at the sea and breathing the salt-laden air, which was probably exactly the preparation and cleansing that I needed for what was about to unfold.

We made our way down to Hobart and decided to eat at a vegetarian cafe. The people working there went out of their way to make us comfortable and had a lovely energy about them. I particularly remember their eyes, which were shining and radiated a peaceful quality. As we were leaving, they invited us to a meeting that night. Just as I noticed a picture on the wall of the man in my dream, they shoved a pamphlet in my hand. My heart skipped a beat as I looked down at the pamphlet—there was the man in my dream again! This had to be fate!

At the meeting, they showed a film of the guru speaking, and I was totally mesmerised by his warm, wise energy as he spoke of finding everything one needed within ourselves. There is never any lasting satisfaction in the external world, he patiently explained; you have to find the love inside yourself. It was the most sensible thing I had ever heard anyone say and I had a magical evening.

We had nowhere organised to stay, and some people at the meeting took us home and put us up for the night. I lived there for twelve months. This was the real beginning of my time of understanding and practising the guru's teachings. It was also the end of my relationship with Michael. It was as though he had come to deliver me to the guru, and once that had happened his work was done. The guru's teachings were to be an integral part of my life for the next fourteen years and still are in a way, but not with the intensity of time and dedication as back then. I learnt so much. I learnt about a place inside myself that is pure love and how to access that place. I learnt about discipline and spirituality. I also learnt that we are all unique and no one is above or below you and we are all special.

The guru was based in America and there were several annual events that provided opportunities to listen to him speak live. In my heart I really wanted to go, and although I had a job waitressing, there was no way I could afford the airfare. At a meeting one evening, a kind friend, Karen, paid my deposit. It was completely Karen's idea. I panicked and told her I didn't know how I could repay her or get the remainder of the airfare.

With a serene smile, she said, 'Just trust, you will be there'. She was right. The money came together effortlessly. I knew I was meant to go.

I travelled to Miami in the USA to see the guru. I was only seventeen, and it was a big deal to me. Never in my wildest dreams did I ever imagine I would get to go overseas at that time. We travelled in a large group, and I felt safe and protected. I found the States overwhelming. It seemed so busy and crowded to me.

The moment I saw my teacher live, I knew all the effort to get there had been worth it. He had a golden aura about him, an indescribable purity and kindness. Being in his presence had a transforming effect on me and a healing on a deep level I could not consciously articulate or understand. I only knew that what he was offering, I needed.

When I returned to Australia, for a short time I lived an ashram lifestyle. We would wake at 5.00 a.m., sing together, and meditate for an hour morning and night. Everyone pooled finances and shared chores, and there was no sex permitted. My memories of this era are of the inner silence of peace I experienced, the sweet scent of sandalwood incense, much laughter, and amazing vegetarian food. Feeling restless, I left Tasmania in 1980 and spent the next few years in Brisbane.

I continued to be involved with the guru's teachings and made a new life in Queensland. I saw an advertisement in the local newspaper for a clairvoyant lady giving readings in the city. This woman was to help me through what were some hard lessons at that time. Another illustration to me of how Spirit puts the right people there at the right time. Her name was Claire and she looked very much like Audrey Hepburn. Claire was not so much a medium as a clairvoyant. Mediums are people communicating with those who have passed, Spirit Guides, or angels. Clairvoyants tune in to your energy and pick up information through their inner senses. Claire could be blatantly honest, and I found her confronting. I realise now it was what I needed at that time. I was making some poor choices in relationships and was confused about my career direction. One week I would be waitressing and the next week cleaning. I was scattering my energy everywhere. I guess I needed a mother figure or a mentor, and in some regards, Claire provided that. I had found a place of peace within, yet I was young and had not learnt how to bring the inner peace into my outer world. I was somehow comforted by Claire's energy.

The last time I ever saw her, as I was leaving, she said, 'You won't see me again; next month you'll move interstate'.

I replied, 'No, I have no plans to go anywhere'.

Claire was correct in her prediction. Quite spontaneously, a month later a girlfriend and I moved to Perth in Western Australia. I never did get to say goodbye to Claire and thank her for the guidance she provided for me at that time.

We had a wonderful time in Perth; it was like a long holiday. After six months, I decided to go back to my hometown of Melbourne. I felt intuitively it was time for me to settle and put my mind to something and learn new skills. It was 1983. I didn't realise then that the next part of the bigger plan for me included marriage.

Chapter 6

Death and Fateful Encounters

My tired legs began to climb the two flights of stairs to my apartment. I had been on my feet all day cleaning at the hospital and was looking forward to having a quiet evening. As I approached the first floor, the sounds of the latest superstar, Sade, singing her hit song 'Smooth Operator' echoed throughout the complex. Somewhere behind the music I could hear a man's voice singing along completely out of tune. It was a tenant from 1A and it made me smile. I found myself humming along.

As I arrived at my front door and fished for the keys in my bag, I suddenly felt very alone. The little girl within me felt like crying at that moment. I was twenty-three years old and had not had a great deal of luck in love. It is clear to me now that I had 'father issues', but at that stage of life, that possibility hadn't occurred to me.

I entered my humble flat, threw my bag on the nearest chair, and automatically inspected the scraps in my refrigerator. It made me feel even lonelier. I reached for the phone and dialled the number for pizza delivery. The pizza employee, Sam, joked that he was expecting my call. As I hung up, I wondered when I would meet someone special and prayed it would be soon.

That evening I was drifting off to sleep when I felt compelled to open my eyes and look at the ceiling. My father's face was clearly superimposed on the ceiling, and although I could hear no words, he seemed like he was trying to speak. Squinting my eyes and shaking my head, the vision remained there for about a minute or so. The vision appeared to be made of a smoky substance. I was not sure what to make of it. I put it down to an active imagination and thought it was time I started sharing a place instead of living alone.

The next morning I was woken by the shrill ringing of the telephone.

It was my mother. 'Sit down', she said. 'I have some bad news. Last night your father passed away'.

I was rather shocked, as I had no idea he was close to dying. Then I remembered his face on the ceiling.

When my father passed, I hadn't seen him for some time. My parents had divorced and had both remarried, and I was closer to my mother than my father. I had heard Dad was unwell, but no one knew how ill until he passed away. At this time I was living alone in a small flat in the inner city, working as a cleaner and studying astrology.

I have heard of other people having similar experiences when someone close to them has just died. I assume perhaps there is a window of time when we pass where we might get a chance to visit our loved ones before we make the transition to Spirit. When a parent dies it has a huge effect on you regardless of the quality of the relationship. I guess we are part of our parents on a cellular level and most likely on spiritual and emotional levels that we may not understand. Although I hadn't seen my father for a while and never had a close relationship with him, his death really affected me. Perhaps the shock was a factor, but more than that it made me go deeper inside myself.

Death makes us question and ponder. It also makes one more aware of one's own mortality.

My father's funeral was a sad affair. It was held in a humble chapel on a rainy day. There were a handful of people there, and only a few of his children attended. As the casket was lowered into the ground, my heart sank with the finality of it all and I felt like I couldn't breathe. It was at that moment his death felt real.

Knowing that I never made a close connection with my father was a sadness that sat deep in my soul. I spent hours trying to remember any profound or special moments that I had spent with him and came up with very little. My mind flashed to a vision of him buying me an ice cream and a memory of him telling me he loved magpie birds. I was grasping at straws. I never heard him say he loved me and never knew what he really felt or thought. It confused me why his death had such a profound effect on me. I came to the conclusion that emotions are not always logical.

Unfinished business is common when someone dies unexpectedly, and this is something I see often in my work. I understand now that there are opportunities to make amends with those who have passed. In fact, these days I have a better relationship with Dad than I did when he was alive, and he has given me some sage advice and reassurance from Spirit at times.

I had another friend, Dylan, who also died around the same time. Dylan came to my flat and complained he didn't feel well, and he did look dreadful. I gave him some aspirin, and as I was in a hurry to get to work, I sort of shooed him out. He died that night in his sleep from a heart attack. I felt guilty I hadn't given him more attention even though I know he is happy now in Spirit.

Those left behind are often filled with guilt when someone passes. I know now with all my heart that Spirit does not want us to feel that burden. If you are suffering from guilt after losing a loved one and plagued with thoughts of 'if only', consider shifting your perspective. If you were the one who had passed into Spirit, would you really want your loved ones carrying a badge of guilt? Release it however you can and replace it with feeling honoured to have known them and to have had them in your life. You may need help to do this, and sometimes our pride gets in the way. If you feel too proud to ask friends, family, or a counsellor, then ask Spirit. You can even ask the person who you have lost to help show you the way to healing.

It was not long after my father had died when a girlfriend, Leanne, invited me to meet a male friend of hers, Ray, who had just arrived from Sydney. Leanne mentioned she was quite attracted to him, and he had recently separated from his girlfriend. She wanted me to come along for moral support.

As we entered the café, African drumbeats bounced from the loudspeakers and partnered with the smell of raisin toast and cocoa. I suddenly felt self-conscious and was glad I had dressed casually in my blue jeans and red T-shirt. Tapping away to the music at a corner table sat my future husband.

Ray was a tall, attractive man with a European background. His long brown hair was pulled back into a ponytail, and he came across as friendly and relaxed. I certainly didn't feel any sparks between us that evening and I know he didn't either. He was a musician and talked about playing and writing music most of the evening, and I had to conceal a few yawns. I made an effort to be inconspicuous and pushed Leanne forward to do most of the talking, as I knew she liked him.

As Leanne and I were walking home, I said totally out of the blue, 'Ray and I would make a beautiful son together'. It was the strangest thing; those words forced their way involuntarily out of my mouth.

Leanne got quite cross with me, as she had already made it clear to back off, and the silly thing was, I wasn't even attracted to him. I apologised profusely to Leanne, but after that she was very cool toward me. I now understand that this sudden verbal outburst was another indication that I was still an undeveloped medium.

The fact is, seven years later I did give birth to Ray's son— who, of course, is beautiful.

Perhaps our son was with us in Spirit that evening. I have often seen people's future children around them in Spirit when reading for them. It makes sense they may have something to do with getting their parents together.

Ray and I became friends at first. We kept running into each other at social events. When he didn't get together with Leanne, I even lined him up on some blind dates, but nothing ever came of them. After almost a year of hanging out as friends, Ray often sleeping on my couch, one day we just took it further. It was a positive experience for me to form a friendship before getting involved. I'd never had that before, and it was a learning curve. We were together almost nine years and married for seven.

My relationship with Ray was to provide me with the stability I was going to need for the next phase of my life. I now see Spirit was setting the scene and putting foundations in place that would help me to be open to their next plan for me. Spirit always knows what we need, even when we don't know ourselves. My unexplained abilities that had haunted me in the peripherals of my soul for many years were about to surface.

Chapter 7

Our Life Purpose

I returned for another session with the amazing medium, Helen. By this time I had grown up a little, studied many spiritual texts, expanded my knowledge of meditation, and my father had passed away since I had last seen Helen.

Again I had to wait a month to get an appointment with her. I understand now that this is the sign of a good medium. If one is that busy, he or she has to be good! I knew it would be worth the wait, so I didn't mind.

When I arrived for my reading, there she was, still in the same dark room with her eyes closed. One might have assumed she had never left since my last visit.

Helen sat peacefully on an old wooden chair. A humble card table beside her held a glass of water and a pink box of tissues. Her hands were folded neatly on her lap, and she would occasionally wriggle in her chair and smooth down her pleated skirt. I waited anxiously for Helen to 'tune in'. I still felt nervous every time I went there. The old hall, and sitting in the dark with drafts all around, only added to the suspenseful atmosphere. My anticipation was growing, and I could sense presences in the room that felt like I could reach out and touch them. I wasn't sure how to articulate or interpret what I felt.

I totally admired this woman in front of me, and I wondered what her life was like outside this room. Was she married? Did she have children? Where did she live? How on earth did she end up doing this? What dedication, I thought, sitting in a gloomy, dark room talking to the deceased when the sun was shining and birds were singing outside.

The reading began, and immediately she said, 'I have a gentleman here who has passed over, who said he is your father'.

My stomach began to tighten as I held my breath wondering what she was going to say next.

'Has your father passed over?' she asked.

'Ah, yes', I replied shakily.

Then she asked me, 'Who is Violet?'

I almost fell off the rickety chair I was sitting on, as that is my mother's name. It also occurred to me that, as Helen had never opened her eyes during my previous visits, she could not have recognised me. Helen definitely did not know I had a father who had passed on. Helen went on to say my father had some unfinished business with my mother and wanted to let me know it really was him. Considering the way we had walked out on him that day when he was at work, I wasn't surprised to hear my parents had unfinished business. Mentioning my mother's name was evidence that totally convinced me it was indeed my father.

Helen said my father wanted to let me know how sorry he was for not being more present as I was growing up. That was an understatement, I thought, as tears began to sting my eyes. I responded angrily, 'Well, so he should be!'

Helen had hit upon a major childhood wound. She was quick to put me in my place. 'Have compassion', she said. 'Your father is trying to make it up to you'.

I didn't feel any compassion in that moment, but I made a decision to be quiet and listen to what else he might want to say.

There were other personal details revealed that Helen could not have possibly known. My father mentioned that he knew I was upset I hadn't been able to get into nursing. He reassured me that my path would reveal itself sooner than I realised. He showed Helen symbols of marriage, and Ray and I had married several months before. I was totally and utterly blown away. As the reading came to a close, something exceptional happened.

Helen opened her eyes and looked into mine. After all these years, in that special moment we finally had eye contact, and I saw such a warmth, light, and love in her wise, hazel eyes.

Helen's slim, wrinkled hand slipped into mine, and she said, 'Dear, you are going to be a great medium. Spirit is insisting that I get you into training'.

I laughed out loud, thinking it was the most absurd thing I had ever heard and said, 'I don't think so. You must be getting your wires crossed'.

Helen laughed sweetly and said, 'Please leave me your telephone number at the desk and I will be in touch'.

A few weeks passed and life went on. I had almost forgotten about the 'me being a medium' thing. Then one day Helen called and said, 'It is most extraordinary. Spirit has been on my back, whispering in my ear every day about you. I want you to contact my friend Joan, who teaches mediumship; she is waiting for your call'.

I held Helen in such high esteem; it may as well have been God on the other end of the telephone, so I felt I had to do whatever she said. I was only twenty-four years old, and although I had a passion for spirituality I found it hard to believe I could do what Helen did—in fact, the thought of it made me downright nervous.

Ray was supportive and said it sounded like a great opportunity and that I owed it to Helen and myself to at least check it out. I summoned some courage and rang Joan. A warm, pleasant voice answered the phone, and after exchanging pleasantries, Joan invited me to come for a cup of tea and a chat. Looking back, I see there was yet another plan unfolding. This is something we often understand after an event but not at the time. It is incidents like these, over the years, that have strengthened my faith in knowing that we are always looked after. I found it interesting that, of all the places in a large city like Melbourne, Joan lived only a few blocks away.

These synchronicities are common when Spirit is trying to get our attention, particularly when it involves our life purpose. Things flow, doors open. If you do not know what your life purpose is yet, ask Spirit from your heart to help you and give you a sign that you will understand.

It was springtime, and the scent of jonquils and wattle flowers filled my nostrils as I walked the few blocks to Joan's house. I had spent an hour working out what to wear. What does one wear to an interview to become a medium? In the end I just went as myself in casual, neat clothes. I found the address I had been given without any trouble—it was a quaint, older-style house with purple flowerbeds in the front garden. I walked up the curved pathway and stood there trying to compose myself. I was about to knock on the door, but before I got the chance the door opened. My eyes met Joan's bright green eyes, which sat behind large round glasses.

Joan was a cuddly woman somewhere in her sixties, who seemed exceptionally normal. Her greying hair was pushed back off her face, and she wore a floral dress. She had an air about her that suggested she was comfortable in her own skin. I am not sure what I expected. Perhaps I thought a medium must be eccentric in some way. My only prior reference was Helen, and she usually sat stationary with her eyes closed.

I think Joan did most of the talking, as I was too nervous, but by the end of the meeting it was somehow arranged that I was to return the following week for my first class. Joan asked me to bring a small item such as a piece of jewellery. There was no explanation of what the item would be used for, and I think I was too scared to ask.

I had no idea at that time where I was going or what I was doing. I had applied twice to begin a career in nursing, and although I had passed the written exam, I had failed the interview process, which involved sitting in front of a board of ten directors firing questions at me. I obviously had the wrong answers to their questions, and I had given up hope of becoming a nurse.

Astrology is a passion of mine, and I had recently completed a course that provided me with a certificate. I was considering doing astrology charts as a second income to my cleaning job. However, passion doesn't always equal confidence, and I felt a huge resistance to actually getting started.

Connecting with Joan was to be the turning point of my whole future direction, and Spirit must have been quite pleased to have manoeuvred me to this point. I myself was in the dark.

Just like that, I was on the beginning of a path that would shape my whole future much more than I knew.

Chapter 8

The Circle

T he September moon was shining, and the stars seemed exceptionally bright as I arrived at Joan's house for my first class. Inside I felt a mix of excitement and nerves. I was worried I would fail and I was worried I would succeed. If I failed I would be embarrassed, but if I succeeded, I was worried what would be expected of me. I only had my gut feeling to go by, and it felt right to be there. I comforted myself with the thought that, so far in my life, my intuition had always proved correct and had at times even kept me from harm. A quiet voice inside me was whispering, 'You'll be fine; there is nothing to fear'.

Joan ushered me into a cosy living room where the only light was a red lamp with a red bulb. The red rays wrapped the room in an incandescent bubble that created a slightly eerie atmosphere. Noticing that I looked somewhat alarmed, Joan patiently explained that the red light helped visiting Spirits to feel comfortable to join us.

'Oh, I see', I replied, trying to sound calm and as though that was totally understandable. My stomach flipped a little as it began to register that Spirits were also being invited to this class.

I was asked to place the opal bracelet I had brought onto a tray and then to cover it with the green satin cloth provided. I did as I was told, having no idea what the tray was about. There was also a list at the door where we could write people's names if they were in need of healing. I wrote down a few names and briefly wondered how doing that could possibly heal anyone.

Joan explained there were three newcomers beginning that evening and that at a later date we would be invited to join the more 'advanced' class. There were four comfortable dining chairs placed in a circle, and within minutes two women who seemed quite normal arrived. One was a friendly, middle-aged woman named Pat, and the other was a sweet young girl, Sue, who looked like she had come straight from working in an office. Apart from the red light there was, so far, nothing out of the ordinary that one might expect at a gathering to talk to dead people.

It was time for the circle to begin. Joan welcomed us and began to explain some ground rules. I began to realise that, as lovely as she was, she also meant business and Joan wasn't going to take any nonsense. 'If you don't follow my instructions implicitly', she said, 'you will be asked to leave the circle'.

I understand now that medium work is an art form, and as with any art form, to achieve a high standard, an element of discipline is required. When people come together with the intention of connecting with the departed or spiritual beings, a better outcome will be achieved if people are in a place of sincerity, respect, and genuine intentions—Joan was not going to settle for anything less.

We held hands as Joan said a prayer of protection and invited our loved ones in Spirit and our Spirit Guides to join us. As I held Sue's hand I felt it shake, and in an odd way it comforted me knowing I wasn't the only one feeling a bit jumpy.

There are many subtleties operating within a development circle.

The prayer and the intention of protection are very important, as they keep the focus on attracting loving and caring energy from Spirit. Having an experienced medium leading the circle is equally important, as their energy is the stabilising element, providing those attending with spiritual protection. Additionally, the medium's energy acts as a conduit to the student's energy, helping activate the students' mediumistic gifts.

Of course at this point I had no understanding of any of this and was simply trusting that this was where I was meant to be.

The list of names of people in need of healing was then read out and a prayer of healing sent. Joan explained this was a form of absent healing and that not only would the recipients benefit, it also helped to set a good-hearted intention for the circle. As she read out each name, we were asked to repeat the name inside ourselves with an intention of love and healing.

Joan then asked us to sit quietly for five minutes and focus on some gentle, healing music that was played. It was also explained that we have seven major energy centres, known as chakras, from the base of the spine up to the crown of the head. Joan instructed that we could open and close these centres in many ways, but tonight we would do this through visualisation. Once opened, apparently we would be more receptive to feeling Spirit energy. As peaceful music began to filter through the room, I began to relax as Joan led us through a brief visualisation exercise to open our chakra centres.

At the time I didn't really understand much about mediumship, but I know now that Joan was attempting to raise the vibration in the room. This is a fundamental necessity for Spirit communication to take place. Spirit exists on a higher vibration than we do. That doesn't mean they are in the sky. Spirit is right here but existing on a different level. For the two worlds to connect, our energy must rise a little whilst Spirit will attempt to come down to match it.

I could literally feel the energy in the room begin to change. My hair began to stand on end, yet by now my fear had subsided. There was an uplifting presence building up in the room. It reminded me of the night I felt energy in my bedroom on the evening we were robbed in the share house. I had no doubt at that point that Spirit had arrived.

When the music finished, Joan explained that the first exercise we were going to do was called 'psychometry', which, she explained, is the art of reading energy from an object and is a wonderful exercise for opening up our psychic senses.

It then became clear that was why I had been asked to bring an item of jewellery. We then each chose an item from the tray. 'Just hold it with your eyes closed and see what images, feelings, impressions, or anything at all you experience', Joan instructed.

I chose a woman's gold watch. Within a moment of picking it up, I sensed a pain in my head and saw mint chocolates. *How bizarre,* I thought, *surely it can't mean anything.* Joan encouraged us to report whatever it was we experienced even if we thought it was crazy. Thank goodness Joan had said that or else I would have kept what I saw to myself.

'Give what you get', Joan encouraged. The logic behind this is that something that may mean nothing to you could be important to someone else.

When it was my turn to share my insights, much to my surprise the owner of the watch knew exactly what I was talking about. Before the class, she had eaten some mint chocolates, and earlier she had taken some painkillers for a headache. This is a perfect example of the difference between a psychic message and a medium message. A medium message comes from a Spirit, usually with some sort of evidential information to accompany the message. A psychic message is picking up information through tuning into a person's energy field. Things they have touched or come into contact with will have their energy around them. I had just received a psychic message.

Pat picked up my opal bracelet and shared that she was shown astrology symbols but she couldn't decipher what they meant. I was able to reassure her that I understood and that I was passionate about astrology.

The next exercise was a medium exercise. Joan explained we were to mentally scan the room until we felt a little tug of energy toward someone. Once we felt that we knew who we were drawn to in the circle, we were to go within and ask our Spirit Guides for help. Then we simply had to wait to see if we could feel, sense, or see anyone in Spirit for this person. I was feeling doubtful about this process and quite out of my depth. The instructions seemed vague, but nevertheless I did what was asked.

I felt a pull of energy toward Pat and then asked my Spirit Guides for help. A vision formed in my mind's eye of a gentleman in his fifties or so who looked European and was pointing to his heart. He then blew a kiss to Pat. Then it was gone. This is not uncommon during Spirit communication, particularly when you are shown images. The image will come in a quick flash, so it takes practice to memorise as much detail as possible.

I decided to try again, and this time felt a pull of energy toward Joan. I asked for help and then I clearly saw a gentleman in his sixties or seventies smiling, standing next to a stack of wheelbarrows, and waving to me. He was dressed in a pair of old-fashioned overalls. When it was time to share our experiences, once again we were encouraged to report whatever we experienced without putting any of our own ideas or interpretations into it.

As it turned out, the first gentleman I saw was Pat's ex-husband, who was European and had died of a heart attack. The second was a relative of Joan's who had passed in his seventies and used to make wheelbarrows. I was so pleased it had worked and it was truly my first conscious experience of working with mediumship.

Sue picked up a medium message for me. She described a short, round older lady, with her hair in a bun, wearing an old-fashioned apron with chooks around her feet. I immediately felt it was my loving grandmother who had passed away several years before.

I realised the beauty of medium work is the evidential information that comes through. The evidential information such as the uncle's wheelbarrows or the husband's heart attack were details that could not have been known. This can potentially bring comfort to people who are experiencing grief and ease fear around one's own death.

The evening ended with a prayer of thanks to Spirit, and Joan asked us to mentally close our chakra centres. She then came to each of us and waved her hands around our bodies, which I honestly thought a bit strange. Joan explained that she was closing down our energy fields before we left so we would not be vulnerable or open to any undesired spirit entities.

It had been an incredible evening, and I had much to think about. I could hardly wait until the next class. It had been very different to the days as a child with Carmen and Doris and the Ouija board. This was not a game but the real thing, and I felt excited and slightly overwhelmed. At that point I still really doubted I could ever be a medium.

Lack of confidence in our own instincts, intuition, and spiritual insight is the biggest barrier for us to overcome when wanting to commune with the Divine. If you are willing to work at it, you can overcome these feelings. Once you make a commitment, you will get much support from Spirit. If you take one step toward connecting with Spirit, they will take a thousand. I say this with full confidence, as I have fallen on my face many times in this work only to be picked up by Spirit, dusted down, and told to keep going.

Every time I do a reading it is like free-falling from a huge cliff. I have no idea what will happen and whether anything I am picking up is relevant, but it's a wonderful learning curve of trust and inner growth as a person and as a soul. The rewards are rich when you know, without doubt, that Spirit has used you as a vessel to help someone else. If I have ever fallen into a mindset that I am someone special or come from a place of ego rather than humility, I have fallen flat on my face. It's wonderful really. Not only does Spirit provide the right teachers for us here, but they also teach you from Spirit. They constantly monitor your progress, provide you with the right information, and guide you with support and encouragement. As with all learning, the lessons are sometimes challenging, but they are all part of the package on the path of living your life purpose.

Eventually, Pat, Sue, and I were given permission from Joan to join the advanced class, which consisted of ten long-term students. The first evening we attended the larger class we were all so anxious. There was no need to worry. We were quickly put at ease by the loving and caring students. Although outside the class none of the circle members had much in common, strong bonds were formed in the class. It helped me learn about acceptance and the power of connecting with others on a spiritual level. I observe that now in the circles that I run. Special friendships are born through a mutual love of Spirit.

I attended Joan's circle regularly for the next four years, and it was over this time that I slowly but surely began to polish my dormant medium skills. Sometimes it was exhilarating and sometimes it was plain depressing. There were nights where I was on a roll and all the information I received from Spirit was well accepted and valid. There were other nights where the only response I received from the recipients of my messages was, 'No, I don't understand that information'. Joan was a tough teacher. She knew too well that if we were going to be serious about working as a medium, we would have to deal with doubting from others and occasional ridicule. In our circle, if you gave a message that was clearly not evidential or was questionable, she would often say something like, 'That was absolute rubbish. Sit down and come back when you have a real message'. They were the nights you wanted to crawl into a shell and never return to circle. However, my love and passion for connecting with Spirit kept me going back, and now I am glad I did.

In my early days of participating in a circle I was fortunate to meet one of my main Spirit Guides, and he works with me to this day. He is White Owl.

Chapter 9

White Owl

'Left hand up and right hand down', Joan instructed as we all held hands around the circle. 'Dear Spirit, we welcome our Spirit Guides and loved ones to join us here tonight. We ask for protection and guidance; thank you, Spirit'. Joan rubbed her eyes and put her glasses back on.

'How lovely to see you all again. Tonight we will be connecting with our Spirit Guides', Joan informed us.

I felt my inner sceptic rise from within. I was open to the concept of Spirit Guides but doubted that I could feel them. I also wondered how you could tell if you were just imagining you had a guide or if it was real.

I posed this question to Joan and she replied, 'In class, we take everything that happens as real, and then you will learn as you go along how to discern fact from fiction; it just takes practice'.

Fair enough, I thought. *I will keep an open mind.* Joan was the teacher, and a student has to learn to trust their teacher, even when one may doubt them. I understood this more when I myself began teaching. The teacher usually has a plan, so the best thing a student can do is be patient and watch it unfold.

The circle had begun in the usual fashion with an opening prayer, group protection, and sending out absent healing. After our meditation, Joan said she wanted to try something different.

We were asked to close our eyes and mentally ask our Spirit Guides to come in close to us. It sounded simple enough, and to be honest, I doubted anything would happen. As I was calling on my Guide to come in close, I was totally taken by surprise. Quite suddenly, it was as though time slowed right down. The room spun a little and I felt nauseous. I opened my eyes and tried to move my body, but I couldn't. Everything was literally in slow motion. It was the weirdest thing. I felt as though I was in a time warp and felt afraid, as I didn't understand what was happening. It briefly occurred to me that perhaps I was having a stroke or a heart attack. It lasted a minute or two and I didn't say anything, as I didn't want to disturb the class. Even if I had tried to talk it would have seemed a huge task at that moment. After what seemed like an eternity but was, in fact, only a few minutes, the strange sensations stopped, and Joan asked us to share what we had experienced.

Thankfully, Joan was able to clarify this experience for me. Apparently, what I had experienced is called being 'overshadowed'. This is when a Spirit comes in too close to your energy field to the point they are overshadowing your space. Sitting in circle and being opened up psychically increased the Guide's capacity to almost step into my body. I understand now that my Guide was trying to align his energy with mine so he could work with me more effectively.

Guides are an instrumental part of medium communication. They are like the mediator between the medium and the client.

Perhaps I should backtrack at this point. What is a Spirit Guide anyway? You can look up many different interpretations for a Spirit Guide, but here is how I see them. Spirit Guides once lived here on earth, perhaps more than once. After they completed a particular lifetime, they chose to stay in Spirit World for an extended period of time rather than hurry back here. Then at some point they volunteered to train as a Spirit Guide. This process would have been an opportunity for them to serve as well as to develop themselves. Once they are ready, the Spirit Guide is assigned to be someone's Guide, perhaps for a lifetime or perhaps for a particular period of time in a human's life. Just as we each have unique gifts, so do Spirit Guides. It is my belief that Spirit Guides are somehow connected to the people they oversee. Maybe they knew each other in another life or maybe they just resonate with each other, but the law of attraction is somewhere at play.

One of the advantages Spirit Guides have is that they have lived here on earth so they are very understanding of the different dilemmas we can experience while in human form. It is common that they have not had a human form for many earth years. This explains why they often present themselves from ancient cultures—for example, tribal elders or Buddhist monks.

With medium work, a Spirit Guide acts as the mediator to connect the two worlds together. The Guide is like a liaison officer communicating with the medium and with Spirit. We all have one or two Spirit Guides from birth until death. However, different Guides will come and go throughout your lifetime, depending on your needs at the time. For example, if you were learning to dance, Spirit might send you a Guide who was a dancer in his or her own lifetime to assist you through to a certain level. Once the assignment is complete, your Guide will move on.

Besides feeling overwhelmed by being overshadowed, that evening I went home feeling no wiser about any of my Spirit Guides. The next morning I had a 6.00 a.m. start at work. I was driving in Melbourne during peak hour traffic and was still waking up. Out of the blue I literally felt a presence sitting first *on* me and then inside my body. I heard a male voice in my head loudly say, 'Good morning, White Owl here'. I simultaneously felt like my physical body was huge, like a balloon that had been blown up inside me. I could sense a presence sitting behind my eyes and looking out. It was different from the night before, as I didn't feel any fear. I wasn't alarmed at all; in fact, I felt incredible peace. I was driving the car, but it didn't feel like me. I felt safe, and a sense of peace enveloped me during the whole drive to work.

I intuitively knew this soul was presenting himself as a Native American Indian. I have always loved their culture, and their belief systems have always resonated with me. As I, or should I say we, pulled into the car park at work, I was all 'me' again. In a flash, White Owl had left. I felt it was his way of introducing himself. I couldn't even share this experience with anyone because it seemed too surreal even to me. It was a good feeling though; I felt a sense of support and hoped he would come back. It was the beginning of a beautiful relationship.

The following week I arrived at my development class to find Joan had invited a psychic artist, Marion, to join our group for one evening. Marion was renowned in Melbourne at the time. Originally she was an artist who then chose to develop her medium ability, blending the two gifts. The result was a unique art form, and I am fortunate to still have in my possession one of her drawings that she did for me.

On this particular evening, Marion was to sit in the corner observing the circle in progress and create a charcoal drawing for each of us of one of our Spirit Guides. As the evening progressed, Marion barely looked at us, engrossed in the work she was doing. Her hands moved swiftly, and my logical mind could not for the life of me work out how she was doing what she did.

At the end of the evening, Marion gave out the sketches to the class members. I was elated but not surprised when she handed me a picture of a beautiful Native American Indian. Marion said, 'He is with you all the time, and as I was drawing him I saw an owl around his head'. I was absolutely thrilled. White Owl had made a huge effort to let me know he was there. Another example of how much we are loved in Spirit. The picture shows a middle-aged Indian with strong features and kind eyes. I was thrilled to now have a visual of the voice I had been hearing.

I later had a private consultation with Marion where she did a beautiful oil painting of another Guide who came through. This time the Spirit Guide presented himself as a Buddhist monk. It was an incredible experience to sit with Marion while she did these drawings. She worked in a semi-trance state, and her eyes seemed to be almost closed. She completed the work quickly, but the end result was very professional. I actually had the oil painting assessed by a professional artist to get his opinion. He said it was very well done and must have taken at least a few hours to complete. I sat with Marion while she painted it and it only took her twenty minutes. When I showed the painting to the appraiser, he said that was impossible! I know now anything is possible.

One fascinating aspect of Spirit Guide paintings is the eyes. They seem to be alive and can change their mood at times. Marion explained that because the paintings are created with psychic energy, they do a have a life about them. The other advantage is having a physical image of your Spirit Guides. It helps one make a more intimate connection with them. I have no doubt these special art forms radiate energy of a healing nature that is very personal to the recipient. There are some wonderful psychic artists available, and I highly recommend seeking one out if you want to make a stronger connection with your Spirit Guides.

Spirit Guides do have their limitations. Unfortunately, they can't wave magic wands and make all the problems in our lives go away. They can't tell us what to do or what choices to make, although they can guide us and make suggestions. There is a lot of work Guides do for us that we are never aware of—Guides will be like a friend to you and comfort you when all seems too much. If you do work in the psychic or spiritual healing fields, they will assist you. Having said that, they will assist anyone with anything where they see fit.

It is possible to build a relationship with your Guides. The main way is through quietening your mind so you can hear them. Rather than call it meditation, which immediately challenges many of us, I like to call it 'quiet time'. Seek out quiet time for yourself, whether it is in nature, in the bath, or simply lying down and daydreaming. Mentally ask them questions. Talk to them and ask for signs. Request your Guides to send you signs in ways you will understand. Spirit will often communicate through our thoughts, so it pays to take notice of any bright ideas or insights, especially when they come out of the blue like a bolt of lightning. It has been said that great inventions began with Spirit placing these ideas into the inventor's head.

If you want to be more aware of your Spirit Guides, there is no mystery. Talk to them mentally or aloud, write to them, meditate on them, and ask them to visit you in your dreams. You can create a garden or an altar in their honour. Give your Guides a chance to connect with you by having faith in your Guides. Most of all, have faith in yourself and your own intuition.

I began to get used to White Owl's presence, and the weird sensations stopped. White Owl's energy was now aligned with me, and my medium work began to improve in class. As I was falling asleep one night, I heard White Owl's voice say, 'Your next assignment will require a leap of faith, but know you will be supported all the way'.

Feeling slightly annoyed I asked in my thoughts, *Why can't you just tell me what you are talking about, White Owl, instead of beating around the bush?* All I heard was the sound of a chuckle in the distance. It wasn't long until the assignment revealed itself.

Chapter 10

Receiving Guidance

When Ray and I married, we moved to the hills. We shared a love of nature and were determined to leave the city madness. The Dandenong Ranges rest on the eastern outskirts of Melbourne. Some believe the East represents illumination. My time there was certainly illuminating in terms of self-growth. Rich green rainforests sit on sacred mountains and radiate an intense energy there. The feeling can be likened to a vortex that draws one in. A friend used to joke that the hills were deep, dark, moist, and womb-like. It really is an apt description.

It was time for change. Ray was playing in a band and working as a gardener, and I was driving for an hour to the city to do cleaning work. I was still training to be a medium. I wanted to create an income locally and had no idea where to start.

Ray and I were having fun in our early days of marriage. We enjoyed an active social life and were content in each other's company. We were excited to move to a more nature-oriented location. It was an easy move. All I did was contact a few real estate agents to let them know we were looking to rent a house in the area. Within days I had a call, and everything fell easily into place. The flow was there, and the timing was right. We moved into our lovely split-level home and celebrated. Surrounded by trees and greenery, my inner senses were at peace, and I had no doubt I was in the right place at the right time. To wake up to birds singing and delicious scents in the air was a novelty and I counted my blessings. We even had an owl that would sit on our balcony every night. I thought perhaps it was White Owl's way of saying he was around.

When I walked down the main street one sunny morning, I noticed a shop for lease. I was incredibly drawn to this shop and stopped to look in the window. I began to see a vision inside my head of it being a spiritual bookshop. I now believe it was Spirit impressing the vision in my mind. It felt like someone was holding my hand that day and I was almost in some kind of light trance. I had always had a passion for books, particularly spiritual books. When I was fifteen I worked at a university bookshop, which was one of my favourite jobs.

Within a day or two, we signed a two-year lease on the shop. In hindsight, it was the craziest thing to do without much thought put into it. I had never run a business before; I didn't even sit down and calculate whether we could afford to cover the essential financial costs. Generally, I am a practical person so I can only assume Spirit was taking over in terms of planning my life at this time.

Ray was supportive of the idea, and we threw ourselves into the challenge. It took us two weeks to find some second-hand fittings, order some stock, and get a basic feel for what we were doing. After some brainstorming, we decided upon the name of the shop. We called it The Self-Discovery Shop.

One busy afternoon, as I was getting organised for our opening, I noticed Ray was talking to a sign writer. I didn't take much notice, as I knew the sign writer had come to paint the name of the shop and the business hours on the shop front.

Later that day I noticed the sign writer had written on the front window 'Astrology Charts by Liz Winter'. I almost had a nervous breakdown! I confronted Ray and practically yelled, 'What the heck is this?'

He replied patiently and firmly, 'No arguments; you can do this'. He was adamant that it was time for me to take astrology seriously, and he was confident I could do it professionally.

As much as I resisted, that was exactly what I needed, a shove in the right direction. I would have procrastinated and kept finding excuses why I couldn't do astrology charts professionally—excuses such as I wasn't ready or wasn't good enough or I needed more time. This is the number-one obstacle I find when teaching psychic development to students. Having confidence and faith in one's own ability is the biggest hurdle to overcome. It is a leap of faith you have to take. It is part of the journey.

The other obstacle for me was that, even though I had lived a colourful life and saw myself as open-minded, societal conditioning influenced me. Buried deep in my subconscious was the belief that you can't actually make money doing something outside the norm. This is where Ray's influence was helpful. Being a musician, he had no trouble believing one could make a living by doing something different. The secret is to just do it. Yes, you will make mistakes as you go along, but you will learn so much. You will also have such wonderful triumphs that warm your heart and feed your soul. If you have a gift to offer the world, my advice is to go for it; the world needs you more than ever now. Just start walking, and let the universe fill in the blanks.

This was the beginning of another phase of my life that set down some wonderful foundations for the future.

We ordered crystals, spiritual books, oracle cards, incense, and oils. I left my cleaning job, and that was the last time I worked for anyone else. It was like a dream come true. I loved being around all those products every day and talking to like-minded people when they came into the shop. For the first time in my life, I was doing something that I felt passionate about. I was also learning about being consistent and responsible. Being accountable for a business was a maturing process for my twenty-six-year-old self.

I believe that once we create something, it takes on a life of its own and emanates its own personal energy. There was a beautiful feeling in the shop that people would often comment on—I am sure they were feeling a strong presence of Spirit. It was 1987, and there seemed to be a surge of interest in spirituality at that time. The shelves were stocked with new-age books by authors such as Sonya Ray, Denise Linn, Louise Hay, and Brian Weiss, to name a few. There were some amazing titles being released around that era that were transforming the way people thought, and I felt blessed to be amongst them.

I began offering astrology charts as a professional service. I would spend hours writing down information and would put a great deal of pressure on myself that it had to be perfect. I approached the local newspaper, and they agreed I could write a weekly 'Stars' column in return for advertising my business. It's amazing how by simply asking sometimes you can get what you want. They published several articles about the shop and about my astrology readings. They made a big deal in one article that I had a computer, a huge clunky thing, which I used to calculate astrology charts. The Internet was not yet available at that time.

Word started to get around about the shop, and we became busier, but it still wasn't enough to cover costs. Within the first few months of opening the shop, the mathematics were not adding up. It was my fault in a way for charging into something and not doing my homework first. There were more expenses than income, and I began to get concerned and had no idea what to do.

There was a beautiful national forest nearby, and one warm summer morning I went for a walk to seek guidance. My heart was heavy, and I felt like the weight of the world was upon my shoulders. Ray was supportive in his own way, but I was the more practical one in our marriage. Golden rays of sun filtered through the thick forest, and the sound of water flowing through the nearby stream began to calm my soul. I often do this when I feel confused or unsure of what to do in my life. Nature has such a calming effect, and it is so much easier to gain clarity and ask for guidance in a natural environment. I spent a few hours walking, meditating, and praying for answers on what to do with the financial mess we were in. After a while I was relieved when I heard the familiar voice of White Owl in my head, 'Do not stress, little one; there is an answer'.

In my mind's eye I saw a sign on our shop window saying, 'Workshops here'. I immediately started arguing with White Owl. 'I can't do that. I'm not ready'.

I was still attending Joan's circle at that point and didn't feel confident to teach astrology. Within seconds I could sense White Owl had left, leaving me to contemplate the advice he had given me.

I reasoned that, seeing I had no solution, I needed to consider the idea White Owl had impressed upon me. I decided that although I wasn't ready, perhaps I could rustle up some people who were willing to teach and I would be the organiser. That is exactly what we did. We ran crystal, tarot, and spiritual healing workshops. I paid the teachers a fee and the students bought merchandise at discounted prices as an added incentive to attend the classes. Spirit seemed to place the right people in front me who were perfect to teach the classes. I created simple flyers and distributed them around the local area and put an advertisement in the local paper. The classes filled up easily.

Within a few months we were out of debt. I met some wonderful people, some of whom I still keep in touch with to this day. I thanked White Owl for his creative solution, and again I had learned several important lessons.

~ Always ask for help.
~ Be prepared to go outside your comfort zone.
~ Don't underestimate your own power when faced with a challenge.

There were some magical moments during our time as shop owners. I recall, after completing a crystal healing workshop, a strange mist filled the room we had been working in all day. We all saw it. It looked like a thin fog that lingered for a half an hour or so. I assume it was Spirit energy and all the healing that had happened during the day had left a mark. We had no digital cameras then and none of us even thought to take a photograph.

Another time Ray and I were crystal gazing. This is when you allow your focus to go soft and flexible while gazing into a crystal. This particular crystal was a clear quartz that had been labelled as a 'record-keeper'. You can identify a record-keeper crystal by the small triangular shapes etched into the surface of the crystal. These are known to hold recorded historic information within them. To be honest, I didn't really believe a crystal could do that and thought it was someone's theory, which I considered a bit 'out there'.

As I gazed into the crystal, I began to see a whole scenario with my eyes open. There was a tribal war going on with spears and people being hurt. It wasn't like watching a colourful movie; it was more like black and white shapes that were distinguishable.

As I watched it unfold, Ray said, 'Wow, look at all those tribal guys with spears'.

'What, you can see it too?' I practically shouted.

That is still an experience I can't explain, but it was something we both saw. I was learning that miracles truly do exist. It seemed Spirit had more miracles for me to witness, and the next one was to come in the form of a medicine pipe.

Chapter 11

The Medicine Pipe

There was a trance medium, Gerard, who ran a healing centre in the hills. (A trance medium is one who allows his or her mind and body to be completely controlled by Spirit.) Joan had recommended him to me, and she believed he was genuine. I must admit I was and still am cynical about trance medium work. How is one to know whether it is real or not?

Joan mentioned there was a meeting coming up at Gerard's healing centre, and she thought I may be interested. When I contacted the healing centre to enquire about the event, the secretary mentioned there was to be a special guest speaker who was a Native American Indian. I had to go! I convinced Ray to come along with me although it wasn't really his thing.

Summer-morning scents filled the car as we drove up the winding mountain road leading to the rustic-looking healing centre. As we got closer, l was in awe of the amazing vista of the valleys below. There was a buzz in the hall where the meeting was being held. I sensed an excitement in the air, and it seemed all eighty seats provided were filling up fast. My intuition knew something special was about to happen.

The Native American Indian, whose name I can't recall, spoke first. He was an interesting and talented speaker and very down to earth. He explained that he had worked on many Hollywood movie sets over the years, and he spoke in a relatable way. When he mentioned he had met John Lennon, Ray was impressed and was now glad he had come along.

The speaker talked about world peace and how we had to go within to find our own tranquility. To conclude his talk, he explained that he was going to perform a medicine pipe ceremony. At the end of the ceremony, he would hold the medicine pipe above his head, and at that point we were all to make a wish. He stressed we should be selective about what we wished for, as it would definitely come true. He spoke with such conviction when he said that our wishes would come true, I totally believed him. He had his audience fascinated.

It was a short but powerful ceremony where he burnt some sage herb and offered prayers to the Great Spirit. Gerard played a drum creating a haunting beat, adding to the anticipation building in the room. Just as the rhythm of the drum synchronised in time with my pounding heart, he held the pipe above his head. The energy in the room felt heightened and full of Spirit, and in that moment, with all my heart, I wished for a healthy baby boy. I didn't plan for that to be my wish; it just emerged from somewhere deep within me. I don't even know why I specified it to be a boy; I wouldn't have cared which sex a child of mine was going to be.

The son I had predicted on that first night I met Ray was conceived in the next few weeks after that ceremony.

During the next part of the meeting, Gerard, the trance medium, was to give a trance demonstration. He explained that he would go quiet for a minute or so and then he would ask his guide, a Native American Indian, to speak through him. He eventually began to speak on spiritual subjects supposedly using the voice of his guide. Feeling doubtful and unconvinced, I started to suspect it wasn't real. Just at that point, Gerard began speaking in a Native American language with expert fluency. What happened next blew my mind. The authentic Native American Indian who had addressed the meeting earlier replied to Gerard in the same language. I knew it wasn't a setup because of the fluency that was coming through in Gerard's speech and intuitively, knew it was authentic. I decided to remain more open to trance work. I myself have never felt drawn to trance work, as I find it hard to let go of control. For some mediums, it is a natural gift. I have witnessed a few other trance demonstrations, but I would have to say Gerard's was the most convincing.

The meetings held at Gerard's healing centre also provided an opportunity for new mediums in training to do platform work (where the medium does a public demonstration, choosing people from the audience and passing on a message for them from Spirit). Much to my disdain, Joan was adamant that her students had to do some platform work as part of their training.

The mere thought of standing up in front of an audience terrified me, never mind trying to get messages from Spirit. However, my teacher was persistent and wouldn't take no for an answer. I begrudgingly turned up at a meeting at Gerard's healing centre one crisp and cool Saturday evening. Again the hall was full. The other students and I huddled together, giving each other moral support. We were all incredibly nervous, as this was our first time outside of the safe confines of circle. We were relieved when Joan took the stage and announced that her students would be making their debut and appealed to the audience to be kind to us.

When it was my turn to take the platform, I was drawn to a woman sitting in the back. I relayed to her that I had a woman in

Spirit who brought forward the name 'Margaret'. I noticed this Spirit was presenting herself wearing a pink cardigan that she kept wrapping around herself. Joan had taught us that occasionally in medium work a Spirit will reveal a gesture he or she had used while living as a way of identifying himself or herself. Remembering that lesson, I relayed to the recipient the way this lady in Spirit was repeatedly wrapping her cardigan around herself. The woman at the back replied, 'No, I don't relate', and then sat down. I felt like hiding under a rock, but I did have one more message for a couple sitting up the front. Clairvoyantly, I could see a little girl in Spirit with a big balloon, and she wanted to send her love to this couple. The couple seemed very excited, and they then shared with me and the audience that they had lost a daughter and it was her birthday that day. A few tears were shed, and they seemed grateful. I felt wonderful that I played a helpful role.

The following week I received a telephone call from Joan. Apparently, the first lady I had received a message for, the one who hadn't related to anything, had subsequently contacted Joan. She asked Joan to relay her apologies to me for saying she didn't understand my message that day. She said she received such a shock that she had been chosen and that the information was so accurate, it had scared her. Not knowing what to do she just denied it and sat down. The recipient of the message said she knew it was her mother—not only because her name was Margaret but because she found it uncanny that I picked up her gesture with the cardigan. This was good news for me and gave me a much-needed boost of confidence.

It is common in a public situation that people often come along to see what it is all about, or perhaps they have lost a loved one and are searching for answers. They don't always have an understanding of medium work. When they actually realise the contact is genuine, it takes time for it to sink in. This is why I have always been so impressed with mediumship. There are no doubts when it is real. Evidential information is one of the key factors with medium work. When a loved one communicating through the medium can give a detail, a name, or a situation that the medium couldn't possibly know, there is no doubt about the authenticity of the contact. This is why it is so helpful for those who are experiencing grief. Even though they can never physically embrace their loved ones again, just knowing they are okay and in a place of peace brings enormous comfort.

My next public appearance was at a suburban spiritualist church. It was a wet Sunday afternoon, and I could have easily stayed curled up on the couch at home. As I parked the car outside the small, quaint church, I noticed people were beginning to arrive for the service and my stomach started to flip. I checked my watch—I had fifteen minutes until the meeting was to begin. The moment I walked in the door, Joan ushered me up front and instructed me to sit and start getting messages before the meeting began. Although I felt quite the reluctant student, I was grateful I had an opportunity to get a head start.

I sat and closed my eyes. I asked White Owl for help and protection. I then heard White Owl clearly say there was a message from a male in Spirit for the person sitting in the back row, three seats to the left. I opened my eyes to get a visual on the person but the seat was empty. *I can't do this*, I thought. Regardless, the male in Spirit carried on with the message that he wanted to give to the non-existent person. I decided to take note of what he said.

The meeting began and had been going for about two minutes when a woman burst through the door looking quite flushed, as though she had been rushing. She sat in the back row, three seats to the left. I was so relieved I could have kissed her. When it was my turn to take the platform, I conveyed the message, and she understood it perfectly. I was learning so much. Trust is one of the biggest things when you are working closely with Spirit. It may look easy to those watching a medium at work, but believe me, it is hard work and often people's expectations are unrealistic. But it can also be richly rewarding, and I wouldn't change it for anything.

If you want a good reading from a medium, here are a few things you can do to help.

~ Go with an open mind and see what happens.

~ If you go with your heart set on a particular person coming through and he or she must give you a code word or a name, you are setting yourself up for disappointment. It may happen but it may not.

~ Keep your body language open. There is nothing worse for the medium than when someone is sitting in front of him or her with arms and legs crossed.

~ Don't try to test the medium, as this often causes confusion, and you will be the one who misses out. If you can't place a name or someone who is coming through, rather than saying no, say you will think about it. This will prevent the energy from waning. To maintain spirit contact, the energy must stay elevated.

People often expect that the only deceased people who are going to come during a reading are those they were close to or knew. This is not always the case. It is not uncommon to get, for example, your great-grandmother, and unless you know something about your family history you may not recognise her. They take an interest in you if you are connected by blood. Imagine yourself in the Spirit World and you heard that your great-grandson was going to see a medium. You would want to put your hand up to be part of the experience. It also gives those in Spirit great pleasure and sometimes healing to be part of a medium reading.

In one circle I taught, a student regularly picked up the name 'Annie' in Spirit for me, and I consistently told her I didn't know an Annie. A year later in idle conversation with my mother, it was revealed that my great-grandmother on my maternal side was called Annie!

One question I am often asked is, 'Does it drain you doing readings?' It can, if you overdo things. I have learnt over the years to pace myself. There was a time when sometimes I would become ill, and it was because I wasn't being diligent enough, protecting and replenishing myself energetically. There are many times when I actually feel energised after giving a reading.

One meeting I attended, I dragged Ray along. I say 'dragged' because he really didn't want to go, but the meeting was in a part of town I was unfamiliar with, and I didn't want to drive there on my own. He finally relented. We arrived late and even though it was winter, Ray sat in the back row wearing his sunglasses. The medium came out to do her platform work. She indicated she wanted to come to the man in the back row with the sunglasses. 'I have a gentleman in Spirit who has passed over who says he is your father and he gives me the letter O' (that was the first letter of Ray's deceased father's name). The lovely silver-haired medium went on to describe a current work situation that Ray was having conflict with and gave wonderful advice on how to handle it.

Ray was flabbergasted and didn't say much on the way home. I knew that day he had a newfound respect for the work I was getting involved in.

I was growing in my medium development and began to let go of resisting my destiny. I had begun to accept this was the path I was being guided along. Spirit and I had come a long way to get to this point.

Then it began. People wanted me to read for them. Although I was scared of failure and unsure if I could serve Spirit well enough, it seemed that this was what I was meant to do. It was time for me to own it.

Chapter 12

I Am a Medium

After undertaking many practice readings, I was beginning to launch my career as a medium. It surprised and fascinated me, time and time again, the information that would come through in a reading. Actually, it still does. For a medium, it is a constant learning curve. You can never rest on your laurels and think you know it all. A true, genuine medium is forever developing.

I created an ambient space at the back of the shop and began taking official bookings for readings. I would play healing music and light candles and incense beforehand in an attempt to raise the vibration. I was a nervous wreck leading up to each appointment, but once the reading began, I would sink into that magical feeling of Spirit energy and wonder what I had been nervous about.

A client, Karen, came to me for a medium reading. Karen was a young mother whom I had never met before. She seemed nervous and sat with her head down, avoiding eye contact. I closed my eyes, asked White Owl for help, protected myself, and opened my chakra centres. I waited. Slowly, a vision of an older woman holding a young baby came into my inner vision. The lady in Spirit presented herself around eighty years of age and wore a straw hat and looked as though she spent time outdoors. She gave me the name 'Lillian' and said to tell Karen that she had the baby with her and that he was doing fine.

As I had been taught to do, I relayed to Karen exactly what had been said without adding my own interpretation of anything. Karen started sobbing loudly, and I waited until she calmed a little. Karen then told me her grandmother was Lillian in Spirit who was an avid gardener. Karen had lost a baby boy the previous year to sudden infant death syndrome. To know her son was with her loving grandmother brought incredible relief for Karen. Although the grief would always be there, it gave Karen immense comfort to know her child was okay.

Ken was a young policeman, and when he first arrived for his reading in full uniform I thought I was in trouble. He apologised and said he was on his way to work after the reading and hoped it didn't distract me. I thought it was quite amusing and proceeded to tune in to Spirit for him. In my mind's eye I saw a young, pretty blonde woman, no older than twenty-five, who was showing me herself dressed in a bridal outfit. Next I sensed a pain in the head and a feeling as though I was falling. Slightly gobsmacked, Ken then explained that he had lost his wife three years earlier when she had an aneurism. It was a tragic love story, as they had only just returned from their honeymoon and were madly in love when she passed.

After three years of depression and grief, he was hoping for his wife to come through and give him permission to move on. He had recently met someone but was avoiding getting too involved, as he felt he was cheating on his wife in Spirit. His wife was so excited to come through and urged him to get on with his life. She told me they had been to Hawaii for their honeymoon, which proved correct and confirmed even more to Ken that it was her.

His wife said she was grateful to have spent the precious, short time she had with Ken. She encouraged him to honour their time together and to keep living his life to the fullest. Ken quickly brushed a tear away and simply nodded in agreement. Ken went on to marry again and start a family knowing he had his wife's blessings.

Not all readings flow as well as these. There are many factors at work when communication between the dead and the living takes place. How the person died and what sort of personality he or she had are major variables. For example, someone who died suddenly, as opposed to someone who knew he or she was dying, may have more unfinished business than the latter. Someone who died suddenly may still be in a state of shock. Someone who was murdered may be angry, or someone who took his or her own life may be riddled with guilt. If the person was an outgoing, talkative type, he or she is likely to be easier to communicate with than a shy, withdrawn person. When someone has been passed over for a long time, the person tends to come through more strongly than ones who are recently passed.

To measure a good reading, I believe you must walk away feeling uplifted. If you walk away feeling drained, angry, or confused, something is wrong. Spirit only wants you to feel their love and their comfort. They want us to know we are not alone on our journey here on earth and that this is like school, and we get to go home at the end. Harsh judgements and condescending advice are not the work of Spirit.

When a young, lively lady named Juanita came to see me, I started picking up information very quickly. A young man of about twenty years of age appeared in my mind's eye, and much to my horror he showed me a gun to his head. He said to tell Juanita he had come to terms with his passing and he held no grudges. He also mentioned a white pushbike. When I related this to Juanita, I was shocked to learn her younger brother had been murdered several years before when he had become involved with drugs and the wrong people. He was last seen riding a white pushbike, and the police found his body in a back alley with a bullet wound to his head, the pushbike by his side. After many tears, Juanita said she was so grateful to connect with her brother and glad he held no remorse, as she wanted more than anything for him to be at peace. Juanita could not wait to play the recording of the session to her mother, who had never recovered from her son's death.

Jason was a middle-aged man who worked as an accountant. He seemed an unlikely candidate to want a medium reading, but who was I to judge? When he arrived I thought he may be difficult to read for, as his body language was closed, his eyes held no joy, and he seemed rather cynical. I don't like trying to prove anything to anyone although I understand why some people are cynical. In a way, you have every right to be until proven otherwise. I prayed extra hard as I prepared myself to read for Jason. It took a while but eventually I had a man in Spirit who felt like his father. However, I was having great trouble getting him to talk. His father had his head down and emanated strong feelings of guilt. He showed me bottles of medication, so I related this to Jason. He seemed quite startled. Yes, his father had passed on, and he had taken his own life through overdosing on his prescribed medicine. There was no doubt it was a suicide. Then the tears began to fill Jason's eyes, and I leaned over to touch his hand. He told me how he and his father had argued a few days before his death. Jason had told him he was sick of his dad being full of self-pity and that he didn't want to see him again. In some way Jason had taken on the guilt and thought he may have pushed his dad to take his own life. The poor man had been carrying this around with him for the last two years.

Finally his dad in Spirit began to talk and wanted to relay to Jason how sorry he was not only for taking his own life, but for not being more loving toward his son. His dad was taking full responsibility for his actions, and as the communication went back and forth from Jason to his dad, unfinished business became more complete. When Jason left that day, he looked like a totally different man from the one who had walked in. No longer were his shoulders hunched over or his expression serious and sad. He had light emanating from his face and a spring in his step.

I have chosen the above examples to illustrate just how healing a genuine medium reading can be. It is often a two-way healing. Those in Spirit are often in need of healing and closure as much as those left behind.

My life as a medium had begun, and I was thrilled the way things were beginning to unfold. After two years of having the shop, it was time to move on. We sold the shop and used the money to put a deposit on a cute timber cottage opposite the national forest. I continued my astrology and readings from home. However, life was about to distract me, and some events were to be catalysts for huge inner growth.

Chapter 13

Dark Night of the Soul

Before Ray and I married, we briefly discussed the issue of children and both agreed we didn't want them. Perhaps because I was the youngest in my family I never had small children around me. I just had no desire to have them. When I turned thirty, I experienced an overwhelming urge to have a child. It hit me like a ton of bricks, completely out of left field. It was not a logical feeling; it was an all-consuming, emotional feeling I couldn't shake. Ray was less than impressed, and it took much persuasion for him to even consider the possibility of having a child. Eventually he relented to a 'see what happens' attitude, and then bingo! I was pregnant. Just as I had wished for at the Medicine Pipe Ceremony, I was carrying a baby boy.

I loved being pregnant. Psychically, I felt the child I was carrying was a peaceful and calm soul. Joan believed the soul enters the body at conception, and I could sense there was more inside me than a growing embryo. I believe expectant mothers do take on the qualities of the child they are carrying. I felt beautiful in a way I had never felt before. My intuition and psychic senses were heightened, and my dreams became vivid. As the months flew by, I began to sense a foreboding feeling, like the moments before a downpour of rain, an anticipation that you can feel but can't touch.

During my pregnancy our marriage began to deteriorate. At first I wasn't concerned, but as it progressively got worse, I realised the relationship was ending, and I was shattered. I naively believed that once you were married that it was for life, and now that I was pregnant, the marriage should be more solid rather than weaker. Maybe it was because the dynamics were changing now there were to be three of us, or perhaps it was just time to move on for new learning. Ray and I had always been socially active, and now that I was pregnant, I went into nesting mode. We became more distant. Ray was playing music late into the night, and I was in bed at 9.00 p.m. We grew further and further apart.

After a twelve-hour labour, our son, Jay, entered the world, and I felt like I had been initiated into womanhood. Giving birth was one of the most intense experiences I have ever known. Jay was born blue and took seven minutes to breathe. It felt like time stopped, and as Ray paced up and down I closed my eyes and prayed.

It seemed our son was contemplating whether he really wanted to be here. I was in a dreamlike state and felt an overwhelming presence of Spirit light up the cold, sterile hospital room. Although it looked grim, I felt calm inside and knew it would be okay. As the doctors worked on Jay, my girlfriend was yelling at him, 'Breathe, baby, breathe', as if she could will the life into him. Perhaps she did. When Jay's cry eventually filled the room, it brought tears of relief to everyone present. The doctors warned me Jay may have problems in the future and would have to be watched closely. I am happy to say that twenty years on, Jay is absolutely fine.

When Jay was eight months old, Ray and I officially separated. We were, thankfully, mature enough to agree that Jay was the priority. We began to co-parent as harmoniously as we could manage. Those early days of our separation are like a blur. I felt numb, shocked, and anxious. I doubted I could be a successful single mother. I was angry because I hadn't put my hand up to be a single parent. This was not how I thought things would be. I began to have panic attacks and started seeing a psychologist. It was the beginning of a long healing journey where I had to address issues that I had long buried. I was learning to accept that sometimes life throws you challenges that you don't see coming. It was an opportunity to heal deep childhood wounds and create a new life, but first I had to get past the resentment and process feelings I had been ignoring. Like a tree in a dark forest that bends to catch the light, I was being forced to stretch and expand who I was.

On the other hand, the pure joy Jay gave me saw me through many of those dark, lonely days. Parenthood is a double-edged sword that elicits the greatest love and the greatest doubt. I did have supportive friends at the time, and as always, Spirit came through for me. Adjusting to the huge transformation of parenthood and separation, I put my work with Spirit on hold.

When Jay was one year old, I felt the urge to get involved again with my work with Spirit. There was a coffee shop down the road and I knew the friendly owners. Jay spent Saturdays with Ray, so I made an arrangement with the coffee shop owners that every Saturday afternoon I would offer readings at their shop. It was a new challenge for me and I was excited. The owners set up a table for me with a thin partition. One thing I hadn't considered was the noise in the coffee shop. Cling, clang, chat, chat, laugh, bang, cling, clang. My first client arrived and I was verging on panic that I wouldn't be able to concentrate. I needn't have worried. As I began to tune in for my first client, I felt a strong sense of peace envelop me, and the outside noises became more distant. I felt the presence of White Owl and others in Spirit begin to build up.

The lady sitting in front of me, Linda, was middle-aged and looked anxious. I sensed a gentleman in Spirit who brought the name Stan and indicated a car accident. He also showed me a wedding ring. He had left behind two sons, and he indicated the younger one was very angry over his father passing. Linda was able to confirm that her husband, whose name was actually Sam, not Stan, had passed six months ago. He was a pedestrian and was hit by a drunk driver. She said their youngest child, a teenage boy, had been a handful ever since. No wonder Linda looked stressed!

Sam was a wonderful communicator, and after the initial emotional release from Linda, he started giving her some great advice. He said to go easy on the boy, as he was hurting. Sam said his son needed someone to listen to him besides Linda, and he recommended that Linda's brother would be a great help to them both right now. Linda said she had thought of going on a holiday to Queensland to visit her brother, taking her son with her. Sam encouraged this and felt it would help. He also suggested they both seek counselling, separately at first and then together later. Sam promised Linda he would be there to help and mentioned to give all his tools in the shed to his sons and to water his rosebush out the back. Linda looked more relaxed when she left. I was so grateful that the reading worked regardless of the cafe noise. It was a crash course in discipline and focus. Now I feel I can read anywhere regardless of what is going on around me.

Time moved on, and before I knew it, Jay had his third birthday. I began to contemplate our future and realised Jay would soon be starting school. I also began to ask myself questions. Did I really want to stay in the hills for Jay's school life? I wanted to be settled for his sake, and I certainly didn't want to take him away from his father. However, something deep inside was nagging me. I could sense it was time for change.

I walked across the road to the national forest one beautiful spring day. Wildflowers were blooming, and the sound of running water from the creek echoed the singing of cheerful birds.

I found a large tree and sat with my back sinking into its comforting trunk. I began to pray with all my heart. 'What is it I should do now, Spirit? What is best for Jay? What is best for me?' After taking some time to find my centre within, I opened my eyes. I literally saw a large orange light in front of me with the face of a beautiful tribal woman hovering in its centre. She was silent, but the orange light then shot into my heart centre. As it did, I felt energised. I didn't understand what had happened. All I knew intuitively is that healing was taking place on some deep level.

I want to explain that I am not the sort of clairvoyant who sees amazing visions like this with my naked eyes often. Occasionally it does happen, and it was one of those special days. After that experience, the thought kept coming into my mind that I should move interstate to Northern New South Wales. This is often how Spirit guides us. If you find yourself getting repetitive thoughts, it is important to take note and not ignore them. Spirit will often drop thoughts into our mind; it is a way of guiding us. When you want to talk to them, think to them—they will hear you! They will also answer you if you have the ears to listen.

I began to ask for signs. This would be a huge relocation for me on all levels. I had a lovely home, friends and family, and Ray was nearby. I mentioned to Ray that if I decided to go, would he be open to moving to Northern NSW so we could continue co-parenting? He went quiet for about thirty seconds and then said, 'Sure I would go'. I was relieved by his response, but still I hesitated and waited.

One weekend I decided to go for a long walk in the forest with a few friends with the intention of receiving signs about my upcoming decision. I was praying hard at that time that if I was meant to make the move I needed clear signs. I had read about vision quests and thought if I put the intention out, I could have my own mini vision quest. I have always been aware that animals crossing your path can be signs, so I made a note to be particularly aware of any animals I might see on our walk.

Halfway through the walk we stopped at a beautiful waterhole to take a breather. As the others were talking amongst themselves, I happened to notice an unusual looking frog perched on a rock nearby. I alerted my friends, and as I did, this frog made a huge leap across the pond. My heart leapt with the frog, and I knew the message was for me. It felt like it was me who had to make a huge leap. I believe you know it is a sign for you when you feel it intuitively.

As we were walking back home, one of my friends, Mitchell, shared with me that he had completed a study on frogs at university. He mentioned that the frog we saw take a leap was a rare species and one would certainly not expect to see such a species in this particular location. That confirmed my gut feeling. I felt as though Mitchell had been there just to let me know the trouble Spirit had gone to for the right sign to come to me. However, I still needed more signs before I was going to commit to such a huge upheaval. I kept praying, 'Please, Spirit, if I am meant to move north, make it clear'. One would think by now I would have 'got it', but I was feeling scared of making such a big change, and being a single mother, I was even more concerned. I was still adjusting to thinking for two instead of one.

Soon after, one night I was settling in for the evening when there was a knock at the door. Standing there was an old friend I had not seen for about ten years. Tim and I had hung out as friends around the time I had met Ray. He was always fun and we laughed a lot. Eventually he moved up to Byron Bay where I was thinking of going. After a big hug and a cup of tea, Tim went on to tell me he was in Melbourne visiting family and friends. He was ready to go back north but had run out of money and was not sure how he was going to get back there. He also said when he got back he was going to need someone to share a house with. Bells started going off in my head. If I did decide to go, there were two things that were bothering me. One major practical detail was how I would get the car up there, as I really didn't want to drive the two thousand kilometres on my own with a young child. Secondly, when I got there, where was I to live? I now had a child to consider, and my backpacking days were well and truly over.

From that night on everything began to fall into place, and I decided that I would relocate to Byron Bay. The money I needed, the tenants for my existing house, and all the details quickly fell into place. Tim drove my car up to Byron Bay, so he got his ride home and secured a rental property for us to share. When Jay and I arrived by plane I had a house to live in and my car waiting. Ray followed us up a month later and settled into the area. The signs could not have been more obvious. This was the beginning of a whole new life in the magical land of Byron Bay.

Chapter 14

A New Beginning

When I think of Byron Bay, I think of freedom to express, rainbows, and the ebb and flow of the sea. Within the area, an electric feeling pervades the senses that may express itself as an epiphany or perhaps as an emotional release. There is a saying that Byron Bay either spits you out or embraces you, and the energy here can be confrontational. In Byron Bay it feels like the darkness meets the light. Perhaps it is the accentuated characteristics of the natural beauty of the area, as it exposes our imperfections and our wounds. Healing is not optional here. You either heal, you leave, or you have a challenging time.

Byron Bay was originally named 'Cavvanbah', which means 'the meeting place', by the Indigenous Australians. The surrounding area is known casually as the 'rainbow region' and the 'alternative' capital in Australia. In the 1970s, hippies and alternative-minded people flooded the region. Its location on the most easterly point of Australia, and the pristine beaches, the subtropical beauty, and its relaxed energy attracts tourists worldwide. There is a certain harmony and tolerance for differences here. Markets and outdoor festivals add to the magical mix. Alternative therapies abound, including energy healing. People hug openly in the street and any style of dress is acceptable, even pyjamas. This makes it a relaxed environment where it truly is okay to be yourself. All these elements come together in a type of collective energy one can feel. It is indeed a healing place.

When I first arrived, the underlying, light-hearted atmosphere was in contrast to the dark, damp forests of the hills where I had come from. The sun seemed exceptionally bright, and I noticed people dressed in bright colours unlike the greys and black apparel of Melbourne.

The large, older-style house Tim and I shared was in the heart of the town and a two-minute walk to the beach. As I was tucking Jay in for the night I could hear live music echoing from the main street mixed with the sound of the waves crashing on the foreshore. I was excited. I could put out my psychic tentacles into the atmosphere and draw on this new, fresh healing energy.

The moving truck bringing our furniture from Melbourne was delayed for the first week, so we lived in a very bare house with just a mattress and a kettle. We ate out and spent all day at the beach. I felt free. The sun was coming out again into my life. It wasn't until I arrived in Byron Bay that I realised how depressed I had been since my marriage breakdown. I found myself sleeping deeply and knew intuitively I was in healing mode. I knew I still had a long way to go, as I still felt resentful about the separation, yet now I could see a ray of light piercing my sadness. I began to feel hopeful about the future, and deep down I sensed impending changes and excitement. The day the furniture arrived my heart sank. Possessions mean responsibility, and it had been fun living simply.

The water in the turquoise ocean was crystal clear and always seemed to be the perfect temperature. As I swam daily, the saltwater washed away old emotional debris. I began to shake off some of the sorrow I had been carrying. The healing energy and deities of the land had opened their arms and embraced me. Each day I felt a little stronger.

I began giving readings in a new-age shop in town. Initially I had been concerned that, as I was new to the area and there were already many readers, I wouldn't have many clients in Byron Bay. My fears were unfounded, as I began to build clientele. I believe your personal vibration will attract the right clients for you regardless of how many others are doing what you do. It seemed there was plenty of room for new-age practitioners. Any previous doubts I had were gone. I was in the right place at the right time.

Looking out to sea while Jay made a sand castle, the thought to begin teaching danced into my mind. It had been a repetitive thought that had been coming into my mind since I had arrived in Byron Bay. Although I had many fears around becoming a teacher, I decided to take the plunge and start my own development circle. I had never taught before but had sat in many circles and knew I could do it. This is the beauty of relocating. It gives one the opportunity to reinvent who you are and what you present to the world. You can be anyone you want to be.

I also remembered a true story I had heard of an artist who decided she wanted to be an art director, although she had never directed before. This lady decided she was going to start telling everyone she was an art director. Before she knew it, she was offered a top position with a prestigious company. How one is perceived in this world can open or close doors, I feel. If you can act it, people will believe it. Inspired by her story, I decided that if anyone asked, I was going to say I was a medium and a spiritual teacher. I also thought by beginning a class it would attract like-minded people and would be an opportunity for me to get some sort of social life in this new phase of my life. One person who came to my first class was to be a truly special friend.

I found a delightful, rustic studio for lease two streets away from my house in a place where I attended a yoga class. I approached the owner, a lovely woman named Celeste who said I was welcome to hire it for my classes. Celeste also mentioned that she and her son, Jono, would love to attend. I placed an advertisement in the local paper and waited. Before I knew it, I had ten eager students.

I was nervous the first night of the class and prayed to Spirit for courage. I arrived early to create an ambience in the room. Lavender fumes filled the air as healing music gently lifted the vibration. Polished timber floors reflected the moonlit windows that displayed a vista of flowers creating a peaceful atmosphere. One by one the students arrived, and at 8.00 p.m. the circle began. I was aware of Celeste's son, Jono. He was a good-looking man about my age with a witty sense of humour. His energy helped me get through the evening. I was blessed by the lovely people who attended.

We meditated and experimented with some psychic exercises, and I answered questions. All went well, and I felt wonderful afterward. Celeste then introduced me formally to Jono. He was an ex-ballet dancer and an extremely creative man. Feeling open to a new relationship at the time, I was slightly disappointed Jono was gay. That didn't stop me feeling immediately connected to him, and he felt the same. He sweetly invited me to lunch at his home the following week and I accepted.

Although in many ways my life was looking up, I still had a lot of inner healing to do. I was still struggling to accept the role of a single mother. There is a saying that what you resist, persists. Once we can accept a situation, things become easier. Although Ray was around, I felt it was ultimately up to me to make sure all of Jay's needs were met. Of course only now in hindsight I understand I was resisting. So often in our lives this is the case. Later on we understand where we were, when we can see the bigger picture. At the time all I had were my instincts and a big dose of self-pity.

Not only was Jono to become a special friend, he was to be a profound catalyst for my own heart healing at that time. Only Spirit knew the bigger picture, and sadly, death was part of the plan.

Chapter 15

Jono

Waking up on the day I was to go to my new friend Jono's house for lunch, I felt older than my thirty-five years. I looked in the mirror and saw dark lines under my eyes coupled with a lack of joy. *What must others see?* I idly thought. *An average thirty-something single mum who looks jaded and insecure?* It was how I felt, and it irked me to think this was so obvious.

Although I was hoping to meet a new partner, I intuitively knew I wasn't ready. Byron Bay and its healing magic were bringing up deep feelings for healing—exposing shadows that had sat in the dark for some time. Feeling like a ship without a mast, I was grateful I had this lunch date arranged. Jay was with his dad, and if not for Jono's kind invitation, I would have stayed in bed all day feeling sorry for myself.

The aroma of garlic bread and homemade soup filled my senses as Jono greeted me at the door with his warm smile and his classic good looks. His hazel eyes, framed by wispy brown hair, always had a hint of mischief about them, and it was impossible not to laugh and smile around him. We chatted about the class and made small talk while he glided around the cosy kitchen, insisting I be waited upon. I relaxed and laughed at Jono's witty jokes. I began to feel the best I had felt for a long time. Spending time with someone where you can let your defences down and just be who you are is such a comfort.

After lunch we went for a walk on the beach and talked about our lives, our past loves, our hopes and dreams. Jono was an amazing and talented man. He had been a member of the Australian Ballet and he had danced before the Prince and Princess of Wales at the Australian Bicentenary. He'd had minor television roles and written and performed in plays. He was obsessed with crystals and loved doing crystal healings and past-life therapy. He was a Reiki healer and was highly intuitive. Every now and then he would say something to me that would go straight to my heart. It was as though he knew me intimately on a level of truth.

During the years I knew Jono, I have never seen anyone speak to people's hearts the way he could. He would confront someone with the truth the person needed to see yet do it with so much love he or she couldn't deny what he was showing. His humour was a pure gift, and he helped me laugh at myself. When I went home that day, I knew in my heart I had been blessed with a friend for life.

As we grew closer, we started seeing more of each other. In a sense it was like we were having a relationship and doing things couples do except have an intimate, physical relationship. He began to show me around the local area and take me to magical locations I was unaware of. One morning he rang me and said, 'Pack up your crystals; we are going on a crystal picnic'. What was a crystal picnic? I wondered. We had a wonderful day. We took all our crystals down to a beach and cleansed them in the saltwater. This is a perfect way to cleanse crystals of negativity. We ate lunch with our crystals and laughed, walked, and talked.

Jono began to speak more honestly to me. He would say things like, 'Liz, you have such a light within you, but you keep choosing to go for the darker thoughts and feelings', or 'You're replaying the hurt from the past; for God's sake, just move on darling, just move on'. I had never had a friend before who could be so candid, and at first I was surprised. When Jono saw the tears in my eyes, he would give me a look of compassion and simply sit with me and hug me while I let it all out. If a friend who genuinely cares about you can confront you with love, it can be the best medicine.

He was absolutely right! I had to move on and stop complaining about what had happened. It had happened; life had thrown me a curve ball, and life tends to do that. It was my choice now how I was going to deal with it. Jono hid all my blues music CDs and said he would give them back when he thought I had lightened up a little. At that time I would often play depressing music and sit and feel sorry for myself. Jono gave me some crystal healings, which were wonderful, and for the first time in a long time, I felt like I was moving forward. Jono gave me a past-life therapy session using crystals, which was amazing. I recalled a life as a mean, young female Egyptian royal who was poisoned, as well as a life in Atlantis where I had known Jono. I saw us both as scientists trying to prove something, but I wasn't sure what we were trying to prove. I attended a few formal counselling sessions and began to feel stronger and more accepting. White Owl visited me and suggested I create a ritual to seal the past and make way for the future.

On a September full moon, in the early evening, I took my wedding ring down to the beach. The tide was high, and as I stood at the water's edge I threw my ring into the ocean. Simultaneously, I said to myself with conviction, 'I now release all the pain and disappointment from my marriage'. The waves hungrily devoured my wedding ring just as the moon rose over the horizon. I was clearly telling the universe that I was ready to move on, and I felt empowered. Rituals can be simple but have a deep impact. It is action marrying intention, which is a mix guaranteed to give results.

One thing I love about working with Spirit is that Spirit has a wonderful sense of humour. I really don't think I could do the work I do if there was not some comic relief along the way.

Jono and I heard there was a 'sweat lodge' with a Native American Indian fellow happening just a few kilometres up the road. A sweat lodge is a cleansing ceremony where a small tent is basically turned into a sauna. There are usually four rounds of sitting in the tent filled with steam, and during each round you are meant to endure the discomfort as you are cleansed and you pray to Spirit. Jono had heard that, as well as the Indian fellow who was known as Paul, there was also another gentleman coming who was called Perry the Pipe Keeper who was apparently gay. Jono and I were both single and hoping to meet someone special in our lives. We started to fantasise how perfect would it be if Paul was just right for me and Perry the Pipe Keeper was right for him. We couldn't think of anything more perfect!

As the sun began to set we drove along the scenic route through the countryside bubbling with excitement and laughter. Jono and I were joking about how we were both about to find our soul mates and checking ourselves in the mirror and laughing. We felt like two children going to Disneyland for the first time.

When we arrived we found Paul, my potential soul mate, in a compromising position with a young lady. Although disappointed, I was still hopeful that Perry the Pipe Keeper would be right for Jono. Eventually Perry the Pipe Keeper appeared. He was about seventy years old. Not that I am ageist, but he was so wrong for Jono. Jono and I couldn't look each other in the eye or else we would have started laughing quite inappropriately. Our romantic dreams went up in a puff of ceremonial smoke; it was back to the drawing board.

It was an education attending the sweat lodge. Paul used a burning sage stick to cleanse our auric fields in a process known as smudging. Then we had to walk in an anticlockwise direction into the tent. As we were doing so I noticed a deadly brown snake waltz by and assumed the spirit of the snake was joining us. From that point on, things became intense.

Inside the tent it was pitch-black. Seven of us had to squeeze into the small tent and our knees were touching. The heat was almost unbearable, and before the first round was over one girl shouted, 'I can't stand it anymore!' and ran screaming naked from the tent. Another woman started moaning, another crying. I had to suppress some giggles when I heard Jono using his super serious tone of voice attempting to calm everyone. It wasn't really funny, but at that moment I saw the ridiculous side of things. Seven naked people sitting in a pitch-black, overheated tent trying to be spiritual, but some were running out naked and screaming. Rather than feeling spiritually uplifting, it felt like a mad house in there. By the time it was finished, there were only a few of us left. I have never had a desire to do another sweat lodge. It was a shemozzle, and it still makes me laugh to this day.

Jono and I had a special bond of friendship, and we kept in touch regularly and continued to do so for many years. Eventually Jono moved south, back to his home town of Sydney.

In 2004, Jono had been complaining of heart palpitations but had not sought medical help, only alternative therapies. In May, he was rehearsing for an upcoming play he had written at a Sydney studio when he abruptly collapsed. He was given CPR immediately from another visitor at the studio. Apparently, he gained consciousness for a moment and smiled, but he then closed his eyes and passed away. He was forty-four, healthy, and fit. The medical reports said it was an arrhythmia of the heart.

When I heard the news, I was numb for days. It was such a huge loss for all who knew him. He brought joy and light wherever he went. I last saw Jono six weeks earlier when he had been visiting the area and I invited him over for lunch. For some reason I brought out the video camera that day and I have him on film laughing and explaining how to read tea leaves. After Jono returned to Sydney, two days before he died, I had a compulsion to call him and tell him I loved him.

I rang his number but his answering machine was on, so I said to the machine, 'Jono, it's Liz. I just want you to know how great it was to see you and tell you I love you'. I will never know to this day whether he received that message. I believe we know on some level when death is near, but perhaps we don't really want to know. I had no dream or warning he was going to die but the compulsion I had, to tell him I loved him, was obviously a knowing within me somewhere. Perhaps you have had similar experiences. I felt Jono's spirit around me soon after he died, and I heard his voice in my ear say, 'Only love is real, that is all that matters in the end'. I have connected with him in dreams and often feel his loving energy around me.

One dream of Jono was vivid and crystal clear—I hugged him and felt his clothes and smelled his scent. I was so excited to see him I started asking him silly questions like, 'Can you eat there in Spirit?'

He replied, slightly exasperated, 'Of course I can eat if I want to, but that is not why I am here. I have come to get you to tell my mother I am with her, and the reason she can't hear or see me is because her grief is blocking it'.

Obviously his mother, Celeste, was having an awful time coming to terms with Jono's death, and this message did help her. Celeste was asking in herself often, 'Jono, please give me a sign you are there'. When I relayed the message from Jono about the grief standing in the way, she knew it was true, but what can one do? You can't control grief. Grief is something one learns to accept and grow through, and often for a parent who has lost a child, it can be a lifelong process.

For Celeste though, it wasn't the first time she had lost a son. In 1953 she had endured another sudden loss. Her young son Peter had drowned. When I first met Celeste at the studio, she booked a reading with me. When I tuned in for her I heard the name Peter and a sense of being engulfed by water. Celeste was stunned; she had been waiting for many years to get some confirmation of her son in Spirit. Peter also wanted to pass on the message to his Dad that he should let go of any guilt feelings he was harbouring about Peter's death. Celeste was able to pass this on, and it enormously helped her husband at the time.

Why someone had to endure losing two children, let alone one, is beyond me. I can only assume there is a higher power and a bigger plan than we can possibly imagine or understand. I do believe we choose our circumstances to a certain extent before we come here. Certain events are pure fate; others are choices we make along the way. The fateful events may include some painful situations. When we make these choices, we are making them from the perspective of what would best serve our soul development. I know one thing for sure: when someone dies it has a ripple effect of deep, inner transformation for all who knew and loved the person who has passed.

The learning gained through grief and loss can be profound. It automatically makes us aware of our own mortality and helps us appreciate our lives and the people we love. If any of you have ever been present at the death of a loved one or even a beloved pet, you may have felt a spiritual presence. It is similar to being at a birth—the entry into and the exit from this world is where angels gather to assist the transition, and we can be witnesses to that high vibration.

When Jono was still alive, he visited me one evening and outdid himself in terms of accurate prophecy. We decided to give each other a reading with the intention of getting a message regarding our love lives. In Jono's reading for me he said, 'I get the name "Dean"; it has something to do with your future'. I filed the information in the back of my mind.

It was only a few months before I met my second husband, Dean.

Chapter 16

Soul Mates

It was late 1997, and I had been living in Byron Bay for eighteen months. Little did I know my whole life was about to dramatically change. At the time, I could not see how. I had built up some clientele, classes were going well, and Jay had started preschool. Jay and I were now living on our own in a small flat in town. Two areas of my life were still a major struggle—one was finances and the other was love.

I wanted more than anything to meet a soul mate to settle down with. I wanted Jay to have a family environment and perhaps for him to have a brother or sister. I was thirty-six, and if all that was to happen, it had to be soon. I felt I had worked hard on my issues around relationships and was ready to meet someone special. Nothing much was happening besides the occasional date that never led anywhere.

Financially, I was struggling. The high rent I was paying on my own and the fact that my work was coming in unpredictable waves was worrying. At one point I had to seek assistance through a charity organisation to help pay my power bill. One Saturday

I was so broke I decided to have a spontaneous garage sale. I gathered up some junk around the flat, took it out to the nature strip, and within an hour I had made sixty dollars, which paid for our food for the next week. Lessons from childhood of being resourceful had come in handy once again.

I started to write in a journal, which helped me gain clarity and work out what power I had to make the changes I wanted in my life. Way back when I was sixteen, at my psychic development class I had learned about the law of attraction. Visualisation, clarity, prayer, and affirmations all help attract what you want into your life. I made a decision that I was going to put these tools into action.

First I started writing affirmations about self-worth. I knew if I didn't love myself enough, then how would someone else love me? I have also learnt with affirmations not to give up on them too easily because it takes time to reprogram our thoughts. I would write things like, 'I, Liz, am worthy of love', and 'I, Liz, now accept a soul mate into my life'. I also started writing down qualities I would like to attract in a partner. I wanted a man who liked children and who was faithful and loyal. My journal became my Bible, and I would read from it every day. I would make adjustments and write about the issues I was struggling with. I was using writing as a healing tool. During my meditations, I started visualising myself looking happy, healthy, and loved.

I had some knowledge about feng shui and discovered that the love area in my bedroom was the far right-hand corner. I placed a table there with some pink velvet cloth and created a 'love' altar. I placed fresh flowers, affirmations, and an oil burner on it. I cut a photograph from a magazine of a gentle-looking man pushing a child on a swing. That was what I wanted: a gentle, loving family man who was honourable and loyal.

Some of my favourite affirmations at that time were, 'I attract my soul mate now', and 'My partner is loyal and loving'.

I placed written affirmations on the refrigerator so I would be reminded. When I went for walks I would take my journal and sit on the beach and rewrite the affirmations over and over. I was determined I was going to find my soul mate and Jay was going to have a step-dad.

One night I had just put Jay to bed and I was lying on the couch feeling particularly flat. *Another night alone,* I thought. Rather dramatically, I said aloud, 'Why, Spirit? If you love me so much, why am I so alone?' At that moment I heard the familiar voice in my head of my lovely Aunt Mary who had passed on, saying, 'Remember when you were at school and maths was your weakest subject?'

I replied, without thinking that this was weird or unusual, 'Yes'.

Aunt Mary continued. 'Life on earth is like that, in the sense that we all come to work on our weaknesses. Part of your learning has been about being on your own. That doesn't mean it is forever; in fact, if I was you, I would get my party shoes ready'. Then the voice was gone. *Come back,* I thought, but no, I could tell the energy had gone, and I was left to ponder her wise words. It had me intrigued about the party shoes! That night I fell asleep somehow comforted by Aunt Mary's visit.

Now the interesting thing is, Aunt Mary's youngest daughter Wendy and I are similar in age. Although we grew up in separate States and didn't see much of each other, we always had fun as cousins when we did get together. Until I moved to Byron Bay I had not seen Wendy for many years. It turned out she was living only an hour away from my new home, and at this point I was just beginning to get to know her again.

The next day after the visit from Aunt Mary, the phone rang. There is a saying that one phone call (one letter, one e-mail) can change your life—this was one of those days. I answered the phone.

'Hi, Liz, it's Wendy. I'm having a divorce party next week; I would love you and Jay to come. By the way, there are going to be a couple of lovely single men there, so you just never know'.

'I would love to come', I said. As I hung up, I had a deep, intuitive feeling in my stomach something was happening here. Was this what Aunt Mary had meant about getting my party shoes ready?

The week passed quickly, and before I knew it the day of the party arrived. Although I had seen Wendy several times since moving north, she had always visited me, so this was to be my first visit to her house.

When Jay and I arrived a few hours before the party, I was overwhelmed by the photographs of my family members on the walls. My dear grandparents, Aunt Mary, and others who had passed on looking down at me made me immediately feel like I was at home. It was then that I began to get a feeling building up in the pit of my stomach. You may know that feeling of anticipation and a knowing that something is about to happen.

Wendy had set up a lovely outdoor area for the party with tables of delicious food and comfortable chairs. When I first walked outside to the patio, a gust of wind came from out of nowhere and lifted my dress. In that moment I heard Aunt Mary's voice inside my head say, 'You are about to meet someone who is going to change your life'. I wanted to believe what I felt was unfolding here, but I was almost too afraid, in case I was wrong, and then I would have to deal with yet another disappointment in love.

The evening began and people started to arrive. After a few hours I had met some nice people, but certainly no one of any romantic interest. I decided perhaps it had been wishful thinking and I may as well make the most of the evening and support Wendy by helping in the kitchen.

Then it happened.

Two men arrived through a side gate carrying a refrigerator Wendy had asked them to bring for extra room for drinks. The first man I saw had his back to me, and all I could see was long dark hair tied back in a ponytail. As they placed the fridge on the ground, I saw his face. My heart dropped into my stomach, and I got a rush in my head. In that moment I knew this person was someone I had to know. I felt an instant connection and an instant attraction.

However, as is often the case with women, I was way ahead of him. He hadn't even noticed me yet.

I spent the rest of the evening trying to be 'cool'.

Wendy introduced us. 'Liz, this is Dean, and Dean, this is my cousin Liz'.

Oh my God, I thought. Jono! Jono had mentioned the name Dean would be important to me—was this the Dean he'd been picking up on?

We were both shy and didn't really talk at that point. An hour or so later I noticed Dean was playing table tennis with Jay, who was five years old by that time. Dean had no idea he was playing with his future stepson. I watched from a distance at the way he was joking and laughing with Jay, scoring more points from my perspective every minute.

As the evening waned, there were fewer people, and Dean was talking to a few of his mates so I decided to be bold. I went and sat nearby and joined in the conversation. Dean was warm and friendly, and I immediately liked him. He seemed very real, honest, and down to earth. He told me he was a surfer and how he loved the ocean. Just as we began to get acquainted, his friend, Gazza, stood up and said, 'Come on, Dean, we're going'. My heart sank but he had no choice, as he had come as Gazza's passenger.

Wendy invited them to a picnic at the lake the next day, and Dean said he would try to make it. Dean told me sometime later that he almost hadn't gone to Wendy's party that night but at the last minute had a strong feeling he should go.

After the party was over I felt euphoric. I could sense something had happened that I didn't fully understand but it was important. Little did I know it wasn't going to be easy.

The next day we made our way to the picnic, and I was so excited hoping I would see Dean again. He didn't show up and I was disappointed, as I assumed Dean wasn't feeling the same connection as I did. I thought I must have imagined it all. I felt all I had now was trust. My future felt uncertain, and all I wanted was to be settled, safe, and secure and to give Jay the best life I could. I also wanted to give more energy to my work but felt it was impossible being faced with basic survival issues such as income and where to live.

Wendy invited me back to her house the following weekend. I accepted, hoping to see Dean again. I arrived on a Friday night, and Wendy and her partner took me to the local pub. I spotted Dean sitting with some of his friends. Our eyes met, and I was instantly reminded of the chemistry I had felt that first night.

After some initial awkwardness between us, we began to chat and talked all night. The body language, the eye contact, and the flirting began. He came back with us to Wendy's house where we were discreetly left alone. I kept saying to myself, *Whatever you do, Liz, don't sleep with him yet. It never works if you do that.* Whether we had too many drinks at the pub, whether it was the stars aligning that evening, or whether it was because it felt like the most natural thing in the world to do, we ended up sleeping together. Even though it felt wonderful and amazing, as soon as it was over an awful awkwardness set in, like 'hang on, we don't even know each other'. I knew I should not have let it happen! Dean left at 3.00 a.m., and I lay awake for the rest of the night trying to work out what had just happened.

There were no phone calls the next day, or the next weeks for that matter, and I felt I had blown a potential soul mate relationship.

A few weeks later Wendy kindly invited me to come and live with her for a while. I took her up on the offer because I could save money, and her three sons would be good company for Jay. Of course it was also in the back of my mind that Dean lived nearby, but it wasn't the only reason I wanted to go. It was Christmas time, and the day after we moved in, Wendy and her family left for two weeks' vacation, so Jay and I were left to housesit and adjust to our new environment.

Wendy had a large family home on a large block of land tucked away behind the town of Murwillumbah in a lovely country setting.

I awoke to hear the family leaving to go on vacation, and I had a mild anxiety attack. I was awake instantly and alert. What was I doing here in this unfamiliar environment? I was to be here all alone for the next two weeks knowing no one! (Except for Dean, who was acting elusive.) There would be just Jay and me, and I felt panicky. At that moment a clear, turquoise-blue light flashed in front of my eyes. I instinctively knew it was either a Spirit Guide or an angel bringing a sense of overwhelming peace and a knowing that all was well. Then I heard White Owl's words in my head, 'Trust, little one, trust'. I took a deep breath; it was all going to be okay, I told myself.

That day I took Jay into town. The sun was burning the pavement. The suntanned crowds were dressed in shorts, singlets, and summer dresses. It was a few days until Christmas, and the streets were jammed with people doing last-minute shopping. There was an excitement in the air, and the streets were scattered with shiny Christmas decorations. Several Santas were ringing bells and giving out sweets. Jay was having a wonderful time taking in all the colour and excitement.

I needed some cash and found an ATM. Waiting in line, I realised the guy in front of me was Dean! My heart started racing and my mind started spinning. *What do I say?* I tapped him gently on the shoulder. 'Hi', I said, as I involuntarily broke into a smile.

We made eye contact and for what seemed like a long moment, and there was warmth as we connected. Then he seemed a bit uncomfortable, as though he didn't want to be there, so we didn't talk for long. I said I was taking Jay down to the local swimming pool, and he said he might come down and say hello. Three hours later I was still at the pool, no Dean. He clearly was not interested in me, I said to myself with a heavy heart. I'd really blown it that night. *The mystery has gone for him; men like a chase,* I reasoned. My mind kept going around in circles trying to analyse the situation. Still this nagging, deep intuition kept saying, '*He is your soul mate*', and then my logical mind would interrupt and say '*in your dreams*'.

Christmas came and went and the days dragged by. I had a couple of visitors here and there but still no Dean. What was worse was that I had to drive past his house to get to town and would see his car there but knew I had no place in his life. I wanted to knock on his door but didn't have the courage. I didn't want to seem like a stalker.

I was walking Wendy's dog one morning and felt the presence of a Scottish man in Spirit walking with me. I suspect he was a guide sent to me around that time because I had never seen him before or since that time. He was lovely and upbeat and kept reassuring me in his lyrical, Scottish accent that all was well. Spirit had a plan, he said, and I would look back at this time in the future and understand what was really going on. How true those words were. He would often come on these walks with me and tell me I would have another child and I had a lovely family life ahead. I just could not see practically at that time how any of that could happen.

It is not uncommon for Spirit to send a guide or helper to assist us at a particular point in time. It is as though the Spirit is given an assignment, and once completed moves on.

About a week after Christmas I was so bored and lonely I decided to ring Dean. I reasoned that I hadn't stalked him or chased him up to this point, so how could a friendly, neighbourly phone call hurt? I was almost relieved when his flatmate Gazza picked up the phone. He was a friendly Aussie guy, and before I knew it he had invited me out with him, Dean, and a few other people that evening to the local pub. I offered to be the designated driver, as I wasn't interested in drinking and he seemed pleased. He said to come to their house about 7.00 p.m. I still hadn't spoken to Dean.

Just play it cool, I thought. *Go with the flow and don't try to force anything.*

I was so excited and spent the rest of the day giving myself a makeover and preparing for the night ahead. Jay was away with his dad, so it was perfect timing. I arrived just after 7.00 p.m. to their house for the first time. It was an old Queenslander set in the middle of sugar cane fields and had spectacular views of mountains, including the famous and magical Mount Warning. I nervously approached the front door and thought how wonderful the cane fields and the mountain views looked at sunset. Gazza answered the door with a friendly smile.

When I entered the house, my first impression was that this was a boy's house. There were three men living in this house, and it looked like it. There was definitely no feminine energy in there at all. It was tidy, but there was no love or warmth in the house. These guys were real men-unlike my previous partners who were sensitive souls, usually musicians. They worked hard, liked a beer, liked their sport, and in a nutshell seemed like true Aussies. Part of me panicked. In my expectations, my future partner was going to be a spiritually aware person, perhaps a healer or a psychic. I wondered there and then if I was just acting out of insecurity and that I had this whole idea of Dean being someone special all wrong. I felt sadness and loneliness in this house, almost darkness, and I began to wonder what I was doing there.

I entered the lounge room, and there was Dean. As usual my heart jumped a beat, and I felt a rush to my head. What was it this guy did to me? I only had to be in the same room with him, and I was reduced to jelly. I mustered all the 'coolness' I could as I noticed how hot and sexy he looked. I hoped my mascara wasn't smudged or I wasn't too easy to read. He was friendly enough but slightly guarded. We made small talk amongst ourselves and then made our way into town.

When we arrived at the pub I wondered why they even wanted to come. It seemed quiet in contrast to the night life in Byron Bay. The whole town seemed asleep for a Saturday night. Of course I didn't care; I was just excited to be there in the same space as Dean. It was that night we began to talk, really talk. Halfway through the night he said to me, 'Look, I really liked what we did that night, but I think we jumped the gun. Could we start again?'

After I picked my stomach up off the floor, trying to stay cool, I said, 'Yes, I would like that'. I think I fell in love at that moment. I thought it was so honest and sweet.

We decided to get to know each other better and leave the sex part out of it. That lasted approximately four hours, and then we spent the night together. This time it was special and deep and didn't feel weird afterward. Still, there was more I had to get through before I would feel safe in Dean's arms.

When we awoke in the morning, he had closed down toward me again. Was it me, was I bad in bed, did he not like me, did he just want sex, did he really mean it about starting over? It was one of those awkward moments when you first begin an intimate relationship with someone yet you don't know them well enough to be bluntly honest or demanding. He basically got up, said a quick goodbye, and was out the door.

Alone again, I lay in bed pondering and reminiscing about the previous evening. My analytical mind went into overdrive trying to work out where this guy was at. He was an Aquarian star sign, I reasoned; they are aloof and eccentric. Dean had been talking about getting a job interstate, so was it for that reason he was holding back? I couldn't seem to get the answers from Spirit, as I was just too attached to the outcome.

Another week dragged by with no word. Wendy and her family came home, and it was time to enrol Jay into school. Life was moving on and not a word from Dean. Part of me began to get annoyed. Why couldn't he just say what was on his mind?

I found the courage to go around his place. When I arrived he was lying in bed with a toothache, but he seemed pleased to see me and was quite friendly. He even kissed me goodbye. After that visit, there was no word, no call, nothing. Hot, cold, hot, cold—I really didn't know what to make of it. Unless I approached him, nothing was happening.

I went into deep retreat within myself. I came to a decision that this whole thing was doing my head in and I had Jay to think about. I had to somehow begin to build a future for us whether it included a partner or not. I had to move forward. No more pining, hoping, or going over to his house. It was time to move on. I ignored the nagging, deep-down feeling that there was more to come with Dean.

About a week later I was riding my pushbike past his house, saw his car there, and had an overwhelming urge to go inside. It was as though my guides were telling me to go inside. I circled around and around arguing with myself. One last time I will see him and will know for sure. I nervously approached the house wondering what sort of mood I would find him in. When he opened the door he broke into a broad smile and warmly ushered me inside. I felt that familiar rush he always seemed to elicit from me.

'How about a cup of tea?' he offered, and I noticed how the light from the kitchen window highlighted his eyes making one look green while the other looked brown.

'That would be lovely'. I smiled. I looked around and noticed that the place looked clean for the boys' house it was and made a comment about it.

'Gazza's been at it again, he really is the house slave around here', Dean mused.

We sat at the kitchen table and had a cup of tea, chatting away easily. We talked about superficial things. I was definitely not going to bring up anything deep and meaningful—I didn't trust what I might say. At that point I was feeling a myriad of conflicting emotions. I felt an irresistible attraction to Dean, yet at the same time I had to be responsible for Jay and be practical. Part of me had let go of the possibility of Dean and I being anything serious, and although I was disappointed I was determined to not let it beat me. Life would go on, and I knew deep down I had a lot to do.

Halfway through the cup of tea, Dean ever-so-casually said, 'So, what are you doing this weekend?'

I said, 'I'm off to Byron. Jay is going to his dad's, so I thought I'd go catch up with a few people'.

'Do you need a lift?'

Actually, I didn't. I had already arranged transport, as my old car had recently died and gone to heaven. In that moment it was almost like I was out of my body watching the whole scene in slow motion, and I said really casually, 'Yes, that would be great, thanks'.

Dean smiled and seemed pleased. His face wore the look a man gets when his team scores a goal.

When I cycled home I felt high as a kite on love and hope. I was finally able to embrace the nagging intuition that there was something special between Dean and me. I knew he had turned a corner and it felt good.

That weekend we never made it to Byron Bay; we stopped at a beach on the way, booked into a motel, and had a romantic weekend. The next few weeks we saw each other often and were having a wonderful time. We were falling in love.

Dean let me know he was going away to Western Australia to work and could not guarantee how long he would be gone. This had been a huge factor in his reticent behaviour toward me. Finally he opened up to me and told me he had an ex-wife. He had been working away interstate, and she had fallen in love with somebody else, and this was why he feared getting involved with me, knowing he was going away again. I reassured him I was going to commit to him and would be loyal. Dean went off to work in Western Australia. He was due back in six weeks for a one-week break.

Just before he left he said, 'Here's some money. Go rent us a house by the ocean'.

That is exactly what happened next.

Chapter 17

Soul Mates in Love

The grey slate floor felt cool beneath my feet as I carried the steaming, crispy bacon and eggs outside to the balcony where Dean sat watching the surf.

'Another whale!' he said. 'That's the tenth one this morning'. Dean was completely in his element.

When he had asked me to rent a house by the ocean, he was half-joking. Well, at least about the ocean part. However, once he left for Western Australia and I put my focus on finding a house for Dean, Jay, and me, this one had fallen effortlessly in my lap. It was a gorgeous two-level home with fantastic ocean views. Dean could walk down a track to go surfing, and we would wake to ocean breezes and amazing views. I saw it as a gift of celebration of Dean's and my union, from Spirit.

It was lonely when he was away working, but I felt pleased the way it was all working out.

On one of his visits home, Dean asked me to give him a reading. Part of me was reluctant, as I always am when I read for people close to me. This is because I already know too much about them and fear it will interfere with the information coming through from Spirit. However, intuitively it felt right, so we went to the office I had created downstairs. Dean was open to spiritual matters and wanted to know more.

As I tuned in for him, I saw an older lady in Spirit who I sensed was a grandmother, but instead of hearing words I was hearing a song. The song was called 'Sadie, the Cleaning Lady'. I thought this was strange, but having had many odd experiences I knew it was best to give what you get in a reading rather than trying too hard to make sense out of it. Feeling slightly silly, I passed on what I was hearing to Dean.

His eyes grew larger, and he looked a little pale. 'You're kidding!' he said. 'That is my grandmother Sadie, who practically bought me up; that song was a joke between us'. Sadie sent her love while Dean was still trying to get his head around what was happening.

Then I had a middle-aged gentleman present himself in Spirit to me. He said he used to work with Dean and his name was John. I passed this information on to Dean and he said he couldn't place this man. I relayed this to the man in Spirit and he said to tell Dean he had a shitty job. When I told Dean what he had said, he burst into laughter. 'Oh, John who used to clean the toilets at work, I forgot about him; yes, he did pass over'.

That reading was enough to convert Dean to a total belief in the afterlife. He shared with me later that all his life he had possessed a great fear of death and would get heart palpitations just thinking about it. Now he had no fear and was very grateful.

After six months, Dean's work finished in Western Australia, and he picked up work closer to home. After we had been together for about twelve months, we were lying in bed reading one night, and I felt a strong Spirit presence around. I put my book down and closed my eyes.

Through my gift of clairaudience (that is, 'hearing Spirit'), I heard a woman's voice. She said, 'This is Sadie, and I want to tell you that if Dean doesn't have a child of his own, he will never grow up'.

I had thought of having another child, but the relationship was still reasonably new, and I didn't want to force anything. I did want a sibling for Jay, who was now six, and I was thirty-seven. I decided to tell Dean that his grandmother Sadie had visited and the message she had bought.

He laughed and said, 'Well, Sadie is probably right; she always was'.

We talked late into the night about our hopes and fears around having a child. We came to a decision that I would stop using contraception, and if it was meant to be, it would be. I reasoned that I had not had a child for six years and was a bit older, so it may take time. It seems Sadie and my future son were perhaps working together in Spirit that night because that very night our son was conceived. Dean and I were surprised at the speedy conception but also delighted.

Our son Ethan was born a healthy, nine-pound boy after a drama-free birth at Byron Bay Hospital. It was the Year of the Dragon, the year 2000. A new era in my life had begun, and I felt blessed. I finally had the partner and the family I had always wanted.

My psychic work went on the shelf, but by the time Ethan was one, it felt right to start doing readings and teaching again. I hired a room out the back of a florist shop. Clients had to walk through the flowers to get to my office, and it was a beautiful time where I made some lovely connections.

Life went on, and then I came to another crossroad where it was time to give myself more attention.

Luckily, Divine help from the angels was close at hand.

Chapter 18

For the Love of Angels

For many years I was cynical about angels and quietly doubted their existence. This was rather ironic considering I was a medium. Back in the 1970s and '80s, no one talked about angels. There was an unspoken feeling that they were out of our league. Then in the 1990s there seemed to be more interest. I read several good books on the subject but was still not totally convinced. I had no doubts about talking to deceased people or Spirit Guides, but I had never had a direct experience with an angel. It wasn't until I had a major health scare in 2006 that I was visited by angels, which ended any cynical ideas I had.

For several months I kept hearing a voice in my head saying, 'There is something wrong with your throat. Get it checked'. Being a busy mother, doing many readings and teaching, I chose to ignore the voice in my head. I felt fine, I had no symptoms.

During a medium development class, a student picked up a message for me. She said, 'I am getting a message you need to get your throat checked'. My heart fell into my stomach; I now knew this was important.

So with my heart in my mouth I went to the local doctor. I asked for a throat scan. At first the doctor was reluctant to give me the referral, as I had no visible symptoms. Exasperated, I told him I 'had a feeling' something wasn't right and eventually he signed the papers I needed for further exploration. Sure enough I had a one-centimetre cancerous growth on the left side of my thyroid gland, which required urgent surgery.

When I visit that doctor's surgery now, they often say, 'Oh, you're the lady who had a feeling'.

At the age of forty-five, I was stunned. I thought I was in reasonable health and was unhappy I would lose half my thyroid, possibly all of it, and be on medication for the rest of my life. I began to pray as you do when you are unsure what is ahead and wondering whether you are going to be there for your children as they grow up. I know now the angels were listening to my prayers.

As I was waiting for the surgery day to arrive, one Saturday morning Dean had taken the children out, and I sat in front of the television feeling quite despondent. A music video show was on, and I was staring at the television without really watching. A music clip called 'Lips of an Angel' by a band called Hinder came on. I had never heard of them before, but for some reason it caught my attention and I found myself suddenly alert. As I listened to the song, the room began to fill with a golden light, and I felt an incredible, loving presence. This energy felt different from people who had passed over or from Spirit Guides. This energy was light, ethereal, and joyful. It was also familiar, like connecting with a friend you hadn't seen for a long time. It is hard for me to describe, but my inner medium knew, deep within, that angels had arrived and that I didn't have to face this fearful experience on my own. My life from that day on began to change. I felt lighter, happier, and more optimistic than I had for some time.

In retrospect I understand now what was happening and why it was happening at that time. I was not growing on a spiritual level. I had become stagnant, even slightly arrogant in the sense that I thought I knew it all. I wasn't learning anything new, and the pressure of surviving financially, caring for a family, and working with people, many of them in crisis, was taking its toll. Being the good Libran woman I am and avoiding conflict at all costs, I was keeping my dissatisfaction inside and not expressing it. That is what the throat chakra and the thyroid gland represents—expression.

There is nothing like a health scare to shake things up and help you to be open to guidance. The angels must have seen that this was perfect timing for me to connect more closely with them. Now I see they had been there all along, but it was me who was not seeing.

The surgery was a success. I only lost half my thyroid and didn't need chemotherapy. Although I was initially put on medication, I healed myself through natural processes to a point I didn't need the medication, and today, my half of a thyroid works perfectly. A special angel called Mary came to me during my hospital stay and saw me through the whole experience. When I woke from the operation, I immediately rang Dean, who couldn't believe how normal I sounded. The doctor seemed almost perplexed that I was talking so clearly, as this is not common so soon after a throat operation.

A week after my discharge from hospital, I entered a competition in a magazine to win a reading with a famous angel expert. I was thrilled when I was contacted to be informed I had won. I needed a lift at that point. It was a short reading, and I was so excited I could hardly speak once the 'angel lady' was there on the telephone. She said I hadn't been clearing myself thoroughly enough after doing my readings and this had contributed to my illness.

She encouraged me to keep on with my medium work and said I was doing some wonderful things. She also said the angels were telling me to write and that I could help people through writing. (It was not long after this I starting writing my column for a local newspaper.)

The angel lady chose an angel oracle card for me, and the card was called 'Apollo', and the key statement was 'Focus upon Your Strengths'. Apollo is the Greek sun god. She recommended I go into the sunlight after each reading, if possible, and ask for cleansing and to be very diligent. It made so much sense, as I have often heard over the years about other mediums with many health problems, and here I was having problems as well.

That same day I went shopping, and when I returned there was a large van parked outside my house with the word 'Apollo' written on it. I guessed it was someone visiting the neighbours, but I knew in my heart it was a sign from the angels to me.

After that, I read every book I could on angels, attended angel workshops, and began running my own angel workshops. Today I use angel therapy techniques in my one-on-one medium readings when I sense it can help someone and have seen some amazing healings take place.

Angels have a higher vibration than Spirit Guides or people who have passed on. When angels are around, you feel a slight change in room temperature, a tingly feeling, or a rush of warmth and love. There is only one golden rule. You must ask for their help, invite them into your life. Angels can only intervene without your permission if it is not your time to pass over. We all have a guardian angel, maybe even more than one, who is with us from birth to death. Then there are the archangels who are in charge of certain areas. For example, Archangel Michael is for protection and Raphael is for healing, and there are many others.

The comfort and the healing angels bring is amazing. Sometimes when we ask the angels for help, the answer we receive may not be as we expect it to be. The angels will respond in a way that is for our highest good. It may be better or different from the outcome we wanted. Also, the angels work in Divine time, not human time. Divine time may be quicker or slower than what we are used to.

Often the angels will show us they are around. It is no coincidence that we see a white feather in an unexpected location after we have asked the angel for assistance. Alternatively, we might hear an angel song on the radio, or see an angel shape in a cloud, or the word 'angel' written in a magazine or as a shop or street sign. This is a sure sign that the angels have heard our request and are acknowledging their presence to us. Sometimes, in times of difficulty or illness, such signs and symbols can be of great comfort.

Once, after leaving an angel workshop and feeling very happy and on a natural high, I decided to go for a walk. As I walked past a coffee shop a little girl about three years old was sitting with her mother at an outside table. The little girl pointed to me and said to her mother loudly, 'Look, Mummy, angels'. Her mother gave me an embarrassed smile, and I just beamed right back. It was confirmation for me that the angels were with me.

I am thankful for my brush with cancer, as I gained so much in terms of wisdom and compassion and it gave me an understanding of what I needed to change in my life. As life settled back down again, it was not long before my relationship status was about to change.

Chapter 19

Reflections

The scent of burning sage filled the air as the shaman, who was also a marriage celebrant, smudged Dean and me. We were married eleven years to the day after we first met at my cousin Wendy's divorce party. We kept it simple and were married in our backyard with family, friends, and a shaman.

It was a windy and warm November day and the presence of our loved ones and Spirit was beautiful. The Scottish guide who had come to me when I was feeling lost and insecure eleven years earlier had been completely correct. Marriage was the icing on the cake.

Since my brush with cancer, not only did Dean and I marry, we bought a home just outside Byron Bay. Jay has now grown into a beautiful young man and is on his way to becoming an IT expert. Ethan is in high school and has a wonderful, witty soul.

Sitting here in my humble home on my laptop, I look up occasionally to the window in front of me. A vibrant green hill scattered with trees and brown cows is framed by a beautiful blue sky with crows flying overhead. I have classes and radio shows to plan and many readings booked. I feel so blessed for the life I have led so far, even the challenging parts.

I have housework to do and still don't know what I am cooking for dinner tonight. Ethan's homework lays untouched on the kitchen table while I eye Jay's jeans that need sewing. Sometimes I worry about my family, I worry about the world, and I worry that I won't finish everything I want to achieve before I die. I guess I am trying to say I am a normal, middle-aged woman living in the 2000s, and just because I can talk to people in Spirit doesn't mean I am any different from you.

I am grateful for this life, grateful for everything that has happened so far. My prayer is that I continue to learn and grow and follow my inner guidance.

In closing, White Owl has a message for you.

'Walk on your path gently, care for yourself so that you can care for others, trust the quiet whispers of your soul, and know that each and every one of you is unique and special. When challenged with fear and conflict, reach out for help and know we are watching; we are here even when you can't feel us'.

This life is short. Life is like a day at school, and at the end of it we get to go home. Embrace it, so when it is your time to go home to Spirit, you will smile and say, 'Thank you, Great Spirit, that time on earth was amazing'.

God bless.